Jesus

A Disciple's Search

MURRAY BODO

Nihil Obstat: Rev. Hilarion Kistner, O.F.M.
                Rev. John J. Jennings

Imprimi Potest: Rev. Jeremy Harrington, O.F.M.
                Provincial

Imprimatur: +James H. Garland, V.G.
                Archdiocese of Cincinnati
                July 8, 1986

Book and cover design by Julie Lonneman.

Illustrations by John Quigley, O.F.M.

SBN 0-86716-064-0

*To my mother and father
in the fiftieth year
of their marriage*

Acknowledgments

The text of this book is printed in sense lines, an ancient form of writing that enables the reader to follow more easily the author's progression of thought line by line, step by step. The credit for drafting the book in this form goes to my friend Susan Saint Sing, who is always the first to read and edit my drafts. She also reorganized this whole book for me when I no longer had the courage to do it one more time.

To her, to my confrere Father John Quigley, who gifted these pages with his illustrations, and to the Franciscan friars I live with who put up with the time I spend away from them writing and dreaming, I am deeply grateful.

The Story of This Book

Five years ago I was reading the Gospel of John and the following passage leaped from the page, fresh and alive, with a significance it had not had before. As so often happens with the Word of God, I felt something powerful move within me, and suddenly Nathanael was very real, a person I somehow recognized.

> The next day [Jesus] wanted to set out for Galilee, but first he came upon Philip. "Follow me," Jesus said to him. Now Philip was from Bethsaida, the same town as Andrew and Peter. Philip sought out Nathanael and told him, "We have found the one Moses spoke of in the law—the prophets, too—Jesus, son of Joseph, from Nazareth." Nathanael's response to that was, "Can anything good come from Nazareth?" and Philip replied, "Come, see for yourself." When Jesus saw Nathanael coming toward him, he remarked: "This man is a true Israelite. There is no guile in him." "How do you know me?" Nathanael asked him. "Before Philip called you," Jesus answered, "I saw you under the fig tree." "Rabbi," said Nathanael, "you are the Son of God; you are the king of Israel." Jesus responded: "Do you believe just because I told you I saw you under the fig tree? You will see much greater things than that."
>
> He went on to tell them, "I solemnly assure you, you shall see the sky opened and the angels of God ascending and descending on the Son of Man." (John 1:43-51)

At that time Jesus seemed removed, absent from my life, and I was trying desperately to find him again, or to do whatever I needed to do for him to find me. I wanted to explore words on the page as a way of being receptive to the Word, but I was afraid of becoming sentimental. I needed a voice to match the voice of my own searching, and that was the voice I heard vibrating in Nathanael's words, "Can anything good come from Nazareth?"

The skepticism, the implied disappointment, almost disgust, that the Messiah he had longed for so deeply should come from a place like Nazareth, fit well my own disillusioned mood. I found in Nathanael a spirit kindred to my own; I found a tone of voice that I hoped would save my scribblings from sentimentality.

And so I began to write, exploring that voice, knowing at the time very little about Nathanael. I had, in fact, never given him much thought before the writing of these pages. And it was not until I had been writing for some time that I began to wonder about the historical Nathanael and who he might be. Much to my surprise, I discovered that Nathanael is only mentioned in two places in the Bible, the passage above and this one, also from the Gospel of John:

> Later, at the Sea of Tiberias, Jesus showed himself to the disciples [once again]. This is how the appearance took place. Assembled were Simon Peter, Thomas ("the Twin"), Nathanael (from Cana in Galilee), Zebedee's sons, and two other disciples. Simon Peter said to them, "I am going out to fish." "We will join you," they replied, and went off to get their boat. All through the night they caught nothing. Just after daybreak Jesus was standing on the shore, though none of the disciples knew it was Jesus. He said to them, "Children, have you caught anything to eat?" "Not a thing," they answered. "Cast your net off to the starboard side," he suggested, "and you will find something." So they made a cast, and took so many fish they could not haul the net in. Then the disciple Jesus loved cried out to Peter, "It is the Lord!" On hearing it was the Lord, Simon Peter threw on some clothes—he was stripped—and jumped into the water.
>
> Meanwhile the other disciples came in the boat, towing the net full of fish. Actually they were not far from land—no more than a hundred yards.
>
> When they landed, they saw a charcoal fire there with a fish laid on it and some bread. "Bring some of the fish you just caught," Jesus told them. Simon Peter went aboard and hauled ashore the net loaded with sizable fish—one hundred fifty-three of them! In spite of the great number, the net was not torn.

"Come and eat your meal," Jesus told them. Not one
of the disciples presumed to inquire, "Who are you?" for
they knew it was the Lord. Jesus came over, took the bread
and gave it to them, and did the same with the fish. This
marked the third time that Jesus appeared to the disciples
after being raised from the dead. (John 21:1-14)

How strange that no other evangelist mentions Nathanael.
Is he for John only an imaginary construct, a symbol of the true
Israelite? Or is he, as some scholars think, the apostle
Bartholomew of the other Gospels? Matthew, Mark and Luke
never mention Nathanael, and John never mentions
Bartholomew. Moreover, in Matthew 10:3 and Mark 3:18, Philip
and Bartholomew are mentioned together, as if they are
connected in the evangelists' minds. This has led some to
believe that Nathanael and Bartholomew are one and the same
person, Bartholomew ("son of Tholmai") being his last name,
and Nathanael ("gift of God") his first. There is no agreement
among scholars, however, and so the true identity of Nathanael
remains one of those historical questions that only time and
scholarship may one day answer.

But as I wrote, I found myself favoring the opinion which
holds they are one and the same person. I remembered the
heroic statue of St. Bartholomew in The Basilica of St. John
Lateran in Rome. He is holding his skin over his arm because,
according to tradition, he was flayed alive. And I remembered
his tomb under the altar of the Franciscan Church of St.
Bartholomew on the Isola Tiberina, the small island in the
Tiber near the great Jewish Synagogue of Rome. Nathanael, of
Cana in Galilee, began to merge on the page into Bartholomew,
the apostle.

Then a couple of coincidences occurred in my reading
that encouraged me to continue writing in the voice and person
of Nathanael. One was my discovery that St. Jerome, writing in
the fourth century, spoke of a Gospel of Bartholomew
consisting of questions Bartholomew puts to Jesus and his
mother Mary before the Ascension. This fact helped me to
believe it plausible that the Nathanael of my imagination would
remember Jesus in the written word. Another refinement of
the voice I was discovering came two years later as I was reading

The Divine Comedy of Dante. At the beginning of the *Paradiso,* the final book of his great poem, Dante calls upon Apollo, god of sun, of light itself:

> Come into my heart, and so breathe
> As you did when you drew Marsyas
> From the skin in which his limbs were enclosed.

Immediately I thought of St. Bartholomew and how he, too, was drawn from his skin. (The Marsyas to whom Dante refers was a satyr who challenged Apollo to a musical contest. He was defeated and skinned alive for his presumption.) Marsyas became a symbol for me of St. Bartholomew who, when skinned, reveals the presumptuous Nathanael, who is the metaphor for my own presumptuous questioning.

And so I huddled beneath an imaginary fig tree near the Sea of Galilee, which I have never seen. I became Nathanael beneath his tree, and he became me and all of us who cannot see Jesus but want to so intensely.

All the time I was writing this book I was involved with a psychologically disturbed person whose healing was the most important thing in my life. And that fact has colored the tone of this book, perhaps even more than the voice of Nathanael within me. I could not understand why Jesus did not just come and work a healing. I prayed and prayed and grew disillusioned. I couldn't explain God's failure to act. My own ideas of who God is, of who Jesus is, were trying to force God to do what I wanted. Then, to quote a contemporary poet,

> As we stand on our dung-heap of ideas and crow,
> He slips away whispering, "I Am," to break bread
> Just when we're discussing his non-existence.
> (Herbert Lomas, *Letters in the Dark)*

And so in the end, I had only to surrender to his Spirit and let Jesus slip away and then emerge to break bread where he chose, rather than where I wanted. I had to let him come, even from Nazareth.

Contents

PROLOGUE

I take as my metaphor, Nathanael:
Nathanael, whose name means "gift of God,"
Nathanael, who might have been the apostle Bartholomew,
or who might have been simply Nathanael,
someone lost in the Bible's pages,
lost in the controversy over his very name.
I become Nathanael in order to remember—
to remember who I am or might become.
But more importantly,
to remember you...

You, Jesus.
Your face in my dreams.
You, standing on the shores of lakes and sides of hills,
your beard ragged and your hair matted
with whatever may have covered the ground
of a night of fitful sleeping.
Your hands rough from the wood of so many years,
your feet caked with dirt and mud,
your clothes dusted with the ever-present sand.

I never forget your eyes upon me,
your eyes and the softness of your mouth,
smiling at all my complexity,
my penchant for strewing confusion
and misunderstanding about me.

How I miss you!
You it was who brought me out,
made it possible for me to believe
I was as good as the others,
to feel my own goodness
rising from within me like Siloe,
a spring of healing water eager to rush outdoors
and spend itself lavishly
on whoever passed my way.

How strange such sentiment sounds,
how unlike me to gush like this about anything.
But that is your power over my powerlessness,
the change you were able to effect in me
because you looked upon me with love,
overlooked what you knew I could not change.

And now I miss you,
because the others, though they love me,
are constantly trying to change me, to make me fit
the icon of who they think we are supposed to be.
And, of course, I do not change
and they grow angry and impatient with me,
and I grow more like I was before.

And so I hope, in this returning,
to somehow reenact what happened
when you walked with us,
standing between me and the others,
a buffer against their disappointment and anger
that I remained stubborn and kept doing things
that made them feel I loved them less than I did.
I never loved them less,
but something perverse in me kept me even from you,

from showing what I have within.

You understood that.
You knew who I was behind my impossible exterior.
But you are no longer here,
and I cannot look into your eyes
and see your acceptance
of who I am,
despite the bitterness that covers my life
like the hard, protective layer of lacquer
you spread over the softness of wood.

And so I remember.
Or try to remember,
for sometimes the memory fades and I cannot see you.
I stop and lean against the mud walls
of an anonymous house I might be passing,
and I feel the fear tightening about my heart
and my pulse pumping wildly
and the dryness of mouth and throat
and the panic that I will slip back to what I was,
that somehow I will lose you.
And I begin to wheeze and wonder:
Is your Spirit trying to leave,
to force his way out of the hollow shell
of what I am afraid I have become?

Sometimes weeks and months pass by
and I cannot find your face,
and then—suddenly, coming around a corner
and meeting a blind or crippled figure
or looking at a slant of light
across a tortured face in the crowd,
I recognize you and reach out to you

and take you in my arms.
And then it begins again,
the criticism and jealousy of those among us
who cannot see your face
in the twisted face I hold in my hands.
They expect it to be made whole
as it so often is for them who pray in your name.

And when it does not happen,
they tell me to leave
and you will make whole without me
what you failed to restore with me.
But I am paralyzed to leave
because I cannot leave you to minister to yourself.
I try to walk away,
but when I turn around to wave,
it is you I see, Lord Jesus,
your eyes upon me,
looking sadly after me walking away from you.
And how can I leave you
who refused to abandon me to the shade
where I sat beneath the tree of my own self-pity?
You refused to give up on who I could become,
on who I already was.
And so I live with all the criticism
and misunderstanding of the others
who love you just as much as I,
but who do not see your face where I see it
because they themselves were never inside
those twisted faces,
as I was.

We find you over and over again, Lord Jesus,
where we ourselves were

when you first found us.
And when we forget to remember
the face we wore when you found us,
then it is that we lose the memory of your countenance.
For your face is our own,
reflected in the faces of those
looking to find your face
in us
whom you have sent as angels,
messengers of the poor God,
whose twisted, tortured body hung
against the evening sky
for all to see what kind of face God wears.

M O R N I N G

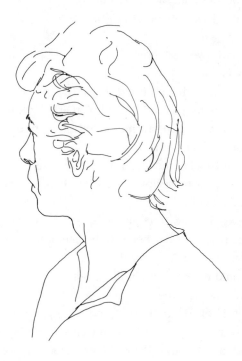

1.

You stood here on the shore of the Sea of Galilee,
the wind blowing through your hair
as it blows now through mine.
You saw me under the fig tree in Cana,
far beyond the reach of human eyes.
What you saw is what I have returned to find,

the reason for this strange life
I've lived these past three years.
I have come back to sort out who I was and who I am,
who you were and who you still are.
You, Lord Jesus, the one from Nazareth.

I know who you are now.
I call you Lord.
I did not then, though I said so glibly,
"Rabbi, you are the Son of God! You are the King of Israel!"
And all because you saw me under the fig tree
and flattered me with,
"Well, an Israelite indeed, in whom there is no guile."
I confess your power over me, even then,
your eyes that saw me,
your eyes that saw through me,
saw my heart that day beneath the fateful tree.
Like Adam I met you after the tree,
as I would meet you again three years later
beneath another tree
on that desolate hill of our abandoning you.
You saw me, too, when I hid in Gethsemane in fear,
beneath an olive tree I would have made my gibbet
had I not seen in the distance
the angels ascending and descending upon you.
I whispered, "Son of Man,"
and remembered your words the day I met you.

Again you had seen:
A seeing that led me to that upper room
where the tongues of fire licked my balding head
and penetrated to the secret of the tree
and I knew that I was forgiven, somehow new,
a child again,

guileless
in the way I wanted to be from the beginning.
The way I really was beneath my sarcasm
when I asked, "Can anything good come from Nazareth?"
The way you knew I was all along.

So here I am, back where we began,
waiting for your hand
to lift me up and lead me back to you
that I might understand
how something so good could have come at all.

2.

I sit now beneath a tree
not unlike the tree where you found me.
Ageless branches rich with figs sigh next to me,
and I remember your words.
I am held in their grip,
hating them at times,
at times clinging to them in a way I wish I needn't.
They cast a spell I cannot shake or explain away.
They are who you are now that you are gone.
And you *are* gone, despite your Spirit.

I suppose your parting is the beginning of faith,
your presence its substitute.
But who am I to try and understand—
I whom you called from the tree of my dreaming,
I who only sat and watched and criticized
the so-called sages

with their convoluted reading of the Law
that turned their eyes inward
until they even looked like men turned inside out?

What is it you said,
"I came to cast fire upon the earth"?
And so you did,
even at your coming as a baby,
a flash of fire upon the straw.
You lit up the cave
from which we all emerge;
you were a flame
that drew people
to the place
where you lay wet and burning
on the manger floor.
And eyes began again to look
outward from the shade of trees,
outward from the tangled brain,
to their Savior, sighted,
focused by a star.

That is what you did for me the day I met you
and heard you call my name:
I began to look outward to you and the One who sent you,
instead of inward to myself.
And even now that we have felt the fire of your Spirit,
my eyes still look outward to the place of your leaving,
to the bright emptiness
your vanishing heels left upon the sky.

I try to lower my eyes
toward those you said were really you
behind the dirt and rags and mouths wagging with hunger;

but the bright space, like your words in my ears,
holds me yet in thrall.
Perhaps this journey backwards
will focus my senses again.
I pray it does not end at the tree
where you found me,
my eyes white from staring into the sun
lest they turn and see the darkness within
that looking upon you turned into light.

3.

Believe me, I recognize how little I have changed.
Still petty and obnoxious
as when I became so indignant
hearing about the sons of Zebedee
wanting to sit at your right and left in the Kingdom.
They didn't even know what the Kingdom was,
but whatever it was,
they weren't going to be left out.
Not them!

And now by some strange alchemy
of Spirit and fire,
I am supposed to join with them
in the grand gesture of preaching your Resurrection.
I who am still struggling with jealousy,
I who am always the last to understand
and when I do,
always seem to give a sarcastic twist to what I know.
How am I going to preach Good News?

How can I be anything but a mockery of what you taught,
a parody of the meek and gentle man
who made me one of his disciples?

There is something ironic in that choice,
almost as if you delighted
in what my tangled mind would make of it.
You couldn't have done worse.
Instead of standing outside the circle of your followers
and criticizing their obtuseness,
I am put on the inside,
aware only of how little like the others I am,
wondering why you have called me
to such an impossible life.
Who are you, Jesus, even now, that you would send *me*?
Humor, I see, survives the tomb.

The others are out gumming the message already
as I sit dumbly by this mottled lake
with its patches of blue and black and green,
trying to understand what *I* am supposed to do,
turning over again those three years
when I was more bemused than serious
about the drama unfolding before me.
It was only for you that I remained,
you who drew me like a seductive woman,
you who were the only sane one of the lot,
you whom I loved and hated simultaneously,
who even now tear my heart.

So how can I speak,
how can I witness to you
when the words that come out
sound satirical, defensive, almost mocking?

What is it, Jesus, that comes between
my guileless heart and my mouth,
so that my words always trip over some quirk in me
before they fall from my lips?

Maybe now, going back to where we began,
I can begin afresh,
start all over again as a child,
try to learn anew how to speak.

4.

I walk along this shore examining the ashes of old fires,
looking for the spot where you sat cooking fish
in the chill of another morning.
Just as that dawn was breaking over the Sea of Galilee,
we saw you standing on the shore
and failed again to recognize you
in the mist rising from the water.

We thought you dead and buried
in Joseph of Arimathea's secure tomb.
We had returned to our boats
and had been all night
on another futile fishing trip with Peter,
who was still able to convince us
that he knew where the fish were.
Every time I got into his boat,
I knew we were in for a long night,
but I could never resist going with him
if for no other reason than his boundless optimism,

no matter how often his nets came up empty.
"They must have moved over here!"
And down would go the nets again into the empty water.

That's why I loved your first words from the shore,
"Children, have you any fish?"
Simon Peter was about to say, "A few,"
when we all shouted,
"Of course not! This is *Simon Peter's* boat."

Then you:
"Cast your net on the right side of the boat,
and you will find some."
You could have told us to cast our nets into the sky,
and Peter would have been convinced
there were fish up there somewhere.
He was so eager to try a new spot,
he didn't even recognize your voice
till John told him what we should have known.
"It is the Lord!"

And he jumped into the sea at his nakedness discovered.
No wonder you loved him so dearly.
He never grasped anything on his own,
but once someone pointed out the obvious to him,
he acted immediately, with the impetuousness of a child.
And his reverence for what was holy
always moved even me
who would have stood there naked,
thinking of what to say
that wouldn't come out with a sharp edge
of sarcasm.

My heart leaped into my throat,
and I stood there gasping for air,
trembling at the thought of meeting you face-to-face
after my cowardice the day of your dying.
How I wished I could be like Peter
swimming toward you,
heedless of his betrayal,
totally intent on seeing you again.
I sat in the boat terrified, ashamed,
thinking of something clever,
something disarming to say.

And again you knew my thoughts
and said what I would have said,
almost in the tone I would have said it:
"Come and have some breakfast."
I almost died of relief.

5.

It was not far from this same shore
that you found me out
the first time I tried my kind of dissembling.
Then and many times between
you let me know you knew
in a way the others never noticed.
You let me be myself,
not because you despaired of my ever changing,
but because you liked me
with my wayward mouth
and my reluctance to be awed by you.

My skepticism somehow pleased you
as if you were challenged and amused
by this hard case of an Israelite
who was always resisting,
who even resisted your cousin John,
that formidable, uncouth ascetic of the wilderness.

How ominous he was
and how ominous was the picture he painted of you.
With his strident voice,
repulsive and at the same time strangely compelling,
with his camel's hair tunic
and his diet of locusts and wild honey,
he stood daily by Jordan's shore
and drew your terrifying portrait:
You were a woodsman wielding an avenging axe,
an angry winnower separating grain from chaff.
Our only escape was to confess our sins,
repent and be baptized.
And we came out by the hundreds
to be regaled and mesmerized by this strange man,
this prophet who assured us
you were already among us,
biding your time.

Like you and like the great prophets of old,
John was speaking for someone other than himself.
The voice of God was rough in him because John was rough.
But it *was* the voice of God, and even I knew it.

What a phenomenon he was,
strutting up and down the riverbank
looking half animal, half water-creature,
waving his arms like some sorcerer

conjuring up visions to convince us of his magical powers.
Were it not for the tongue of God that he had become,
he would have been dismissed as a madman
and been left to rant and rail at the elements and animals
and the images that danced in his head.

But there was no dismissing
this phantom of the human-beast
who lives deep within all of us,
who seems to scream his rising from our loins,
trying to escape through the mouth
into the air and light around us.
I am sure John reminded us of this creature
inside the human heart
who is struggling to be redeemed.
John was a wailing vision
of what it was in us we were denying,
that angry animal who is clothed in camel's hair
and devours the locusts that attack our bread,
who wanders through the wilderness seeking deliverance.

And to some, including me,
John did in fact seem at times no more than a charlatan actor
who had donned the costume of human depravity
to scare us with a living mirror
of who he believed we had become,
the sweet wild honey dripping from our lips
masking the stench of rotting locusts in our bellies.
But even those scribes and Pharisees
who did dismiss him and judge him mad,
showed in the vehemence of their attacks upon him
that he had struck at something vulnerable within them.
And seeing religion's predictable rejection
of this strange prophet,

the common people came in droves
to plunge into the waters
they believed John had made holy
by his fasting and praying,
his fearless reconciliation
with the angry waters inside himself.

Like all beginnings
the baptism of John was simply an admission of sin
and the will to be purified,
to be of those who were being made fit for the Lord.
The Messiah was at last among his people
and those who repented and accepted John's baptism
would recognize him when he chose to reveal himself.
And what is more, a lot of the people believed
the moment of revelation was near at hand.

And so it was, for you were there,
mingling with the crowd, waiting for the fullness of time,
believing that John was indeed your Father's emissary
preparing the way for you.
And even you were drawn to John.
You heard the cadences of your Father's voice
behind the rough and strident cries
of this man of the wilderness.
You saw in his eyes the same driven look
that the demands of the Father's will
had put into your own.
Like you he had been sent, and that was enough.

6.

I seem grafted to this tree.
I don't want to get up, not even to move
into the deeper shade of the eucalyptus grove.
I need to stay rooted, as this tree is rooted,
and remember and think
and piece together everything that led me here.

I look up from staring at the water turtles
that look like little floating loaves of bread;
there is a single feathery cloud in the high heavens,
and there again on the stage of my imagination
is John the Baptist.
I see him standing alone on the riverbank
where he has finally seen the Son of God.
Suddenly you have emerged from the crowd,
as he knew you would,
and then you are gone.

Some say you are in Judea baptizing.
Are you helping John, or sending him signals
that his ministry is now superseded by the one
whose shoes John feels himself unworthy to fasten?
Shortly afterwards the Baptist is arrested,
and he disappears from sight.
And then you say,
"Believe me,
God has raised up no greater son of woman
than John the Baptist."

I am strangely comforted by the fate of John;
I see in it the fate of those who are sent
to preach the Good News of your coming.

When you do in fact reveal yourself to them,
the apostle recedes more and more
into the background of importance in their lives.
John again: "The bride is for the bridegroom;
but the bridegroom's friend,
who stands by and listens to him,
rejoices too,
rejoices at hearing the bridegroom's voice;
and this joy is mine now in full measure.
He must become more and more,
I must become less and less."

And how it did speak, this voice of the Bridegroom!
I was not so much impressed with what you said
when you came uttering the kind of thing we had heard before
about the sun being darkened,
the moon not giving her light
and the stars falling from the sky
as the Son of Man appeared in the clouds
with great power and glory.
Such imagery I had heard from my childhood.
But your commonsense statements took me by surprise:
"If someone sues you,
come to terms with him
while you are both on the way to court;
otherwise he may hand you over to the judge,
and the judge to the constable,
and you may be put in jail."
Not only did words like that show
that you had lived
in the real everyday world
but the emphasis shifted
from cosmic events that Yahweh accomplished
to what we could do,

to what we had to do
to be part of God's Kingdom.
Your very first words were not cosmic but personal:
"The time has come; the Kingdom of God is upon you;
repent, and believe the gospel."

Most, of course, thought your words *were* cosmic,
that the Kingdom of God was some kind of new age
in which God would visibly rule his people.
And so they were disappointed
and disheartened when all they saw
was you doing human acts divinely
and saying they could do the same
if they only had faith.
Everything they had hoped to see was still invisible
and so much of living and coping
still depended on them
more than they wanted it to.

Some, I know, condemn me for saying this,
but I believe our salvation is more our own work
than we want to believe.
Each one of us, in a sense, saves
his or her own world.
We do it only because your death and resurrection
empowers us to do it,
but we do it ourselves just the same.
You gave us the power to save ourselves and our world.

The apocalyptic stuff has been around for a long time;
and when you uttered it, I used to yawn.
But what you learned from your Father
while you worked as a carpenter in Nazareth—
that excited me because it showed me

what the Kingdom of God looks like,
how I could recognize it with my own eyes and ears:
It was always human-looking,
and only what happened to the heart
and how we changed our lives
revealed the divine underside
of the reconciliation that took place on a dusty road
while two people were on their way to court.

Some left you, of course, because they were scandalized
to learn that they still had to do for themselves
what they had hoped you were going to do for them.
They should have known how it would be
when even John was arrested and beheaded.
No avenging Yahweh reached down
and plucked him out of prison.
No divine shield protected him from harm.

Now their Yahweh was again separate,
dissociated from his people,
even from those who proclaimed his justice
and prepared the way for him to reenter
the hearts of his Chosen People.
God did not snatch John from the jaws of death,
because, as we were to learn from you,
it was the jaws of death that enabled John
to become the true precursor of the Messiah.

Death as the passageway to the fullness of life:
I have heard it over and over again
and still I do not want to believe it.
It seems a mere rationalization
to preserve the myth of Yahweh
and explain away the absurdity of faith

in a God who says one thing and does another,
a God who cannot even protect his prophet
from a petty, second-rate princeling like Herod Antipas.
It is precisely here that I falter again and again.
What does it mean that Yahweh saves?
Does it have anything to do with the here and now?
Or is it all a future, apocalyptic event
that rewards a present blind faith in that same future?

Then I realize again how responsible we are
for our own lives and salvation,
that we bring to birth in our own lives
the God who has already saved us.
But we do not know him
until we give birth to him who lies dormant within,
until we surrender to the penetration of the Spirit
in that absurd moment
when, like John, we begin to see
what it means to love God above his creatures.
That, I suppose, is what John knew when he said
he must decrease that you might increase among us.

Viewed from the outside,
what Yahweh let happen to John
is only another example of the "impotence" of God.
What happened *inside* of John
because of his fidelity to an "impotent," "absent" God,
is altogether another story.
John was made pregnant with God,
who is born in us when we embrace the empty air
and find our arms wrapped around ourselves.
God dwells within us,
but we do not know it
until we no longer expect to find him in the air around.

7.

And so you were born from John's dying.
You came into Galilee proclaiming,
"The time has come; the Kingdom of God is upon you."
You spoke in the synagogues
and preached under blue or cloudy skies
that God was near,
that the most urgent necessity of life
was to respond to his presence and become
one of his new people.

A new people becoming:
That was the feel it had for me
when I first saw what was happening all around you,
how you healed bodies and minds,
how you rekindled a faith in Yahweh
that we never thought could return in our time,
how you drew people to yourself
as to an intimacy they had longed for all their lives.
I remember layers and layers of despair
lifting from my heart
when the words of your great poem rang in my ears:

>   Come to me, all you whose work is hard,
>   whose load is heavy;
>   and I will give you relief.
>   Bend your necks to my yoke,
>   and learn from me,
>   for I am gentle and humble-hearted;
>   and your souls will find relief.
>   For my yoke is good to bear,
>   my load is light.

Everything you ever asked of us
is contained in these few astonishing words
that you spoke publicly
but which are heard individually
and require a personal response.
In this request is the paradox
of who you become for those who hear
and then begin to walk with you:
a yoke good to bear, a light load.
But most of us hesitate here
at the center of what seems a contradiction.
We cannot conceive of how the burden of you
can possibly be good and light to bear.
A burden, after all, is a burden;
and that is what we avoid,
what we flee in seeking the freedom
we know is somehow inalienably ours.

The very notion of bending our necks once more,
even to you, is difficult
and filled with centuries of other memories,
of being told by priests and rabbis that we are to submit
and accept all our burdens as Yahweh's "will"
or Yahweh's "just punishment" of our sins,
or "the way" to an ordered Jerusalem.
And now you come saying the same thing,
and even more audaciously asking
that we bend our necks to you personally.
You, then, make yourself the center
of all the ambiguity we feel
about God and religion and the interpretation of the Law.
You make yourself the focus
of all our hopes and dreams and doubts.
You make yourself Messiah.

And there the controversy begins.
There God's death becomes inevitable.
We now have a tangible person
toward whom we can direct
our personal and collective hatred of God
(that we dare not direct to Yahweh),
just as you so dramatically prophesied we would:

> "There was a rich man who planted a vineyard,
> he walled it in,
> dug a wine-press and built a tower in it,
> and then let it out to some vine-dressers,
> while he went on his travels.
> But when the vine-dressers found his son coming to them,
> they said among themselves, 'This is the heir;
> come, let us kill him
> and seize upon the inheritance.'
> And they laid hands on him,
> thrust him out from the vineyard, and killed him."

Once you made yourself the one sent into the vineyard,
the only question that mattered was who sent you.
No one could deny your powers,
but were you savior or sorcerer?
Did your power come from above or below, or both?
Your enemies claimed
that the power of evil itself was in you,
that you could remove it from others
because it came from the same source as your healing.
It was Satan who brought evil into the world,
so he could also remove it through you
in order to advance the credibility of his emissary,
you, the so-called prophet from Nazareth.
Then, in the end, you would be exposed as a false prophet

when, with ignorant people behind you,
you would move against the true faith
of our father Abraham
and all the real prophets after him.

And such persuasion might have worked
even to explain your casting out demons,
were it not for your compassion
for those who had sinned.
You restored people's faith in their own goodness
when you dared to say, "Your sins are forgiven,"
and they in turn believed
they had received Yahweh's forgiveness
when they accepted it from you.
Even your enemies had to admit
that only God could convince us our sins were forgiven.
Your word became our salvation
though we did not know yet
that it would take on flesh and be sacrificed
and eaten that we might have the life
you began promising us already
at the beginning of your preaching.

8.

Why do your words hold me so?
They only raise more questions,
present more problems,
cause at times more pain.
What is it they touched in all of us
that we let everything fall to the ground

and ran almost stupidly after you?
I think I see, and then only dimly,
the depths from which the Word in you emerged,
those depths we have been fleeing all our lives
and which our ancestors fled before us.

Your words rose from that dark cavern of the soul
from which the faith of our fathers
was supposed to save us.
At least it was that way for me.
Until you came, the Law and the prophets
were a thin, fragile crust of safety
over the terrible tunnels of darkness
that wound through the soil of my brain.
And I kept looking to the sky
waiting for Yahweh to send more words,
more prescriptions to strengthen the crust
lest I fall into the bowels of my own Gehenna.

Then, out of the very darkness I feared so much,
you burned through to the surface,
a volcanic, irresistible pressure inside
that shook me like an exorcistic rite.
I closed my eyes
and leaned against the tree and trembled.
And when I opened my eyes again,
you, who seemed to have come from inside my soul,
were standing there before me,
saying you saw me sitting beneath my tree.

Was it from outside you saw
or from inside, or both?
Whatever.
I only know that when you began to speak

I recognized,
like an answering echo, the other side
of the voices that had taunted me
from those caverns of the mind and heart
I had been desperately trying to cover over
with layers of laws and prescriptions,
whose careful requirements fulfilled,
allowed me the self-deception of believing
that what is legally performed
will assuage the demon within.

What a shock it was then,
to discover that the demon within me was you.
Is that too strong, Jesus?
Or is what I am saying
the truth of how you knew me beneath the tree?
The shadow of darkness I feared
was really cast by the laws my own fear set up
between you and the self I was afraid to look at.
Then you stepped out
from behind those walls of my own making,
and I fainted from recognition.

Behind everything about you,
and behind our leaving everything to follow you,
was that something inside and beyond your words
which made us risk believing
you were more than you appeared to be.
The Messiah perhaps,
though that was never so important to me
as it was to most of the others.
For me you were a messenger from that other world
I wanted so much to believe in,
but was afraid existed

only in my desire for it to be,
a mere creation of my own imagination.

I used to sit for hours
and scare myself thinking
about my own mortality.
I would eye the world surrounding Cana
as I am now dreamily turning my eyes
to the mountains that surround the Sea of Galilee—
mountains that are green to the west,
brown and ragged on the eastern shore
where they border the encroaching desert
and, to the north,
the awesome snow-covered heights of Mount Hermon.
And I would touch the soil beneath me
and sniff the air and listen to the wind
in the branches.
What I could see and touch
and hear and smell and taste
was everything there was,
and it would all end for me
when my own senses failed.

And then you came along,
claiming to have seen me
under the tree of my wayward thoughts.
What kind of eyes could see and ears hear
as though from afar
and yet be as near as the neighboring air?
And did they belong to a messenger
from one whose mouth was invisible
and who yet could utter his name from a burning bush?
It was because I believed
you were some kind of angel of the invisible world

that I followed you, Jesus of Nazareth.
Who you really are I never even imagined.
It was enough to risk believing
that what I had dreamed
might, in fact, exist apart from my own mind.

Even now it is hard for me to believe
who you are,
leave alone when you were with us
and would be exhausted and still couldn't sleep
and would toss and turn until daylight.
Or to see you, your eyes full of sleep,
rise before dawn and stumble in the dark
to urinate behind some olive tree.
And we, turning in our dreams,
would see you returning to the cold ground
to wait or maybe even sleep until dawn
when they would come looking for you again,
they with their illnesses and fears,
their demons and brokenness.
And all the time you were surrounded
by a glory we could not see,
just as now that we have seen your glory,
we are beginning to forget the homely features we saw
when you walked the roads with us
and tried to tell us who you are.

9.

I see I can still sit for hours looking
at birds like these black and white kingfishers

and yet not see them because I am looking beyond,
to the desert that lies to the east of the lake—
the desert I keep returning to in reverie.

We tell the story of your temptation in the desert
when we meet to break bread in remembrance,
and each time I hear it,
I grow more certain that anything we might do
to help build up your Kingdom
can only begin with our own confrontation
of the voices that frighten us from within.
Your way of looking honestly into the heart
must be ours.
If our own hearts cannot be redeemed,
then neither can the world around us.
That for me is where faith in you begins,
where your faith in the Father was tested.

We know now that you have saved us from our sins,
but we do not know what that means
or how to live accordingly
unless, like you, we refuse to run
away from the Father's will.
Everything I did not understand in you
hinged on your listening to the Father
instead of to the voices around or within you.
And yet because you listened to him,
you did indeed know how to listen
to those other voices.

My anger when you were among us
stemmed from my wanting to flee
the desert of the Father's will
or wanting you to flee it because it seemed absurd.

And while I was so often angry,
you moved in a deep peace
because of the choice you had made in the desert
and renewed each day thereafter,
to place the will of God
before everything else in your life.
And I know now
(perhaps it has come clear only this moment)
why embracing God's will brings such deep peace:
In that embrace I embrace death.
Not only the idea of death, which everyone must face,
but my own personal death,
with its place and time, as well.

To embrace death is to know no further fear,
for the death-fear is behind everything
that disturbs and troubles our hearts.
Of course, only faith can convince us
of your promise that death brings life.
To believe is to live the Father's words
which you gave us by living them yourself,
and it all began there in that desert
whose hills I can see from where I am now sitting,
watching the white sun threatening death
to all the distant desert creatures
who are hiding in the ground or under the rocks
or in the shade of the few trees
which, like them,
are barely holding on to life.
And I am here, a covering of tree over my head,
trying to overcome my fear
of the life-giving sun that can kill.

10.

Sometimes I think the last idolatry in me
is my own image of myself, my defensive sarcasm.
Perhaps that is the image I should destroy:
the iconoclast destroying his own iconoclasm,
which is perhaps more dangerous
than any image of gold or silver.
The false idol is the image of myself
that I have set up in my heart.
But then, maybe I am only beginning to yield
to the uniformity I detest in some of your followers.
Or do I secretly envy others their sameness of apartness,
the way your disciples
usually sound and act uniformly eccentric?

What would you say, Jesus,
you who once saw me thinking thoughts like these
and responded by saying
that I was a true Israelite without guile?
What on earth were you thinking,
and why did I think you were telling the truth
and not just flattering me?
And what was the guile I was supposed to lack?

It took a long time for me to name
the guilelessness you were talking about
and understand why it was you called me.
I believe your reasons
were tied to the political expectations
that surrounded you
and that moved someone years later
to look back nostalgically from Golgotha and say,
"We had been hoping

that he was the man to liberate Israel."

In me you saw no such expectation,
no secret, political reason for following you.
I, in fact, detested politics
and all the pain and suffering
our preoccupation with freedom from Rome
had brought upon us.
My sarcasm was most often directed
to those whose sole purpose in life seemed to be
to create a Messiah out of anyone
who even remotely looked like someone
who could rally anti-Roman forces around himself.
What a laugh!

Only a misguided faith in a god
whose nature was essentially bellicose
and nearsightedly Jewish
could possibly embark on such a futile enterprise.
And only such a fanatic myopia
could have seen you as the great Liberator,
the age's military genius,
instead of the bread you insisted on being.

You were surrounded by fools
who insisted on circumscribing the soul,
on cutting it off from those mighty images
which reveal its true nature
and turning it instead
into the possession of one nation, one people.
But the soul is more universal
than the nationalism of any local religion,
Rome *or* Jerusalem,
and so you spoke of food

and gave us food
and promised to be food
instead of a shield.
You came to satisfy the hungry soul,
not to satisfy our need for national independence.
But, of course, the food you became
did in fact accomplish
that personal and collective freedom
we thought was won only
with sword and spear and swift horse.

Whenever we cried out for a national solution,
you supplied one that was universal and individual.
You spoke to the individual soul
the message of its own integrity
("a true Israelite" or Roman or Samaritan)
and affirmed its goodness ("without guile")
or not ("you whitened sepulchers, you brood of vipers").
In fact, we were all aware
of your hatred of that hypocrisy
which masked guile with Jewish piety or nationalism.
Only the true hunger of the human heart
deserved your attention and recognized who you were.

That is why you responded
to the five thousand with bread and fishes,
and that is why the crowd was grateful for the food
but did not understand,
especially when you continued to speak
of bread and banquets and ended up by saying,
"The bread that I give is my flesh."
We wanted answers and actions, not the poetry
many of us thought you were uttering.
You were giving us what we really wanted

but we did not know it
because your gift came in a different package
than what we were expecting.

Our expectations of the Messiah
were colored by our own personal and political needs,
so that when you came wrapped in a different color,
we did not recognize you,
and we believed Yahweh had been false
to his own promises.
But, of course, he was only being *true* to his Word.
It was we who could no longer hear it
since we had predetermined what the Word would be
and how it would sound.
We *knew* who God was
and what his prophets would say,
and therefore there could be no surprises,
no initiative from Yahweh himself.
We had defined him and circumscribed him
with names and attributes that fixed forever
how he was supposed to act.
We had surrounded ourselves with laws and proscriptions
whose fulfillment gave us the knowledge
of a God we had created.

Then you came along manifesting the power of Yahweh,
even claiming to be the Son of God,
but we couldn't find you in our own definitions.
We could not conceive of Yahweh
doing or being other than
what the authoritative teaching of religion
had already predetermined.
We knew who Yahweh was
because our religion told us;

so when he began to speak through someone
not officially ordained to speak for him,
when he revealed himself
in a carpenter from Nazareth,
when he began once more to demand faith of us,
our knowledge prevented us from listening.
Only those who did not know
or who repented of their knowledge
could hear the Word of God
or believe the Word could become bread
or human.

11.

And so the lines of battle were drawn,
and they were between you and the established religion.
And the closer you drew to Jerusalem,
that bastion of orthodoxy,
the more certain it became
that the war would in fact be waged.
I remember now with sorrow
your own sad words, "It is unthinkable
for a prophet to meet his death
anywhere but in Jerusalem.
O Jerusalem, Jerusalem,
the city that murders the prophets
and stones the messengers sent to her,
how often have I longed to gather your children,
as a hen gathers her brood under her wings;
but you would not let me.
Look, look! There is your Temple forsaken by God.

And I tell you, you shall never see me
until the time comes when you say,
'Blessings on him who comes in the name of the Lord!'"

It was then you left Galilee,
the encounter with the five thousand
fresh in your mind.
You knew that between you and the Galileans
nothing would ever be the same
because they did not understand about the loaves.
And so you came
into this foreign territory across the Jordan,
and here they could hear you
because they had no preconceived notions
of who you could not be.
And I was comfortable once more.

I was always more comfortable when you crossed
the Jordan and left Galilee.
Maybe it was because of my uneasiness
with my own people and their incessant preoccupation
with the Messiah liberating his people.
(Your own would-be followers were of this ilk.)
That, I'm sure, is why
you had to leave Galilee for a while.
They hadn't understood about the loaves there,
as they could not believe in Nazareth,
and would not repent in Capernaum,
Bethsaida and Chorazin.

And what is worse, the Galileans
were hell-bent on making you king,
on making you the kind of Messiah
you had already rejected.

The people were beginning to rise up,
because they did not listen to what you said;
they only saw your power
and were determined to use it to their advantage.
It was time to retreat,
lest the Galileans compromise
the real nature of your mission.

And so you used your influence over the people
to disperse the crowds peaceably
and you compelled us to take the boat
across the lake at nightfall
with storm clouds already menacing the water.

And I, who am terrified of sea-storms,
rejoiced and jumped into the boat,
relieved at last of the insular concerns of Palestine,
embarking on a voyage of self-discovery
which, though dark and stormy,
was not petty.
And I was happy because you finally saw
what I had seen from the beginning:
Your political use to the people
was much stronger
than the message of love;
and only by repudiating their political interests
could you begin to speak to that deeper dimension,
that human side you came to redeem.

Redeem is probably too strong a word
for what you thought then,
but it is the word we learned later in the upper room
when the tongues of flame burned away
all the personal glosses we had placed upon your words.

What we learned there was that your followers,
we intimates included,
were living and working on a different level from you.
We were working on the level you failed at—
the external level of accomplishment—
whereas you had been working
at another kind of activity, transformation,
a metamorphosis of the soil
that nourished the roots
that flowered into an external configuration
which was supposed to be who we were.
We were concentrating on the flower
while you were working on the soil, *in* the soil.
You were working underground.

12.

Well, I am still here,
staring blankly at the lake I forgot was here—
the same sort of thing I've done all my life,
the very pose you found me in
that day beneath the tree
which even I am beginning to tire of remembering.

And yet, how do I move on?
How do I find your footsteps again,
turn out and away from my own wayward thoughts?
I fear I'm becoming
like the scribes and Pharisees
whose exaggerated self-scrutiny you hated so
because it kept them from the world outside

where God was standing
on the shore of a lake, a river,
and they only saw and heard an error
invading the temple of their minds,
threatening the order their own needs had forced
upon the world outside.
As if hypnotized by their own teaching,
they could not see that nothing matters
but the love of God which is made real
in loving those who threaten to destroy the Temple
they'd built
to preserve their notion of God;
for only in that love are the Law and the prophets fulfilled.

How sad
that we sometimes desperately try to preserve for God
what God himself is trying to destroy.
Anyway, that is what I've learned about myself
these past three years
and that knowledge is for me
the knowledge that leads to salvation:
I must let God destroy in me
the temple I have erected to preserve him
but which only imprisons him
and prevents him from leaving and surprising me
with his presence
where I least expect,
in those whom I despise,
in those who mock the temple
I have built to contain him.

13.

The cranes, hundreds of them,
are passing overhead like a great snowstorm.
The cranes, those white presences I've known all my life,
whose passing reminds me always of other presences,
whose leaving frightened me,
though I knew they had to go.

Always it was the empty house I feared,
that space within swept and clean,
waiting to be occupied by something better
than what was there before.
And how I *did* listen to you for words
that would fill the void
left by the departure of those presences
that were incompatible with following you.

At first
I thought you were going to fill that space for me
or lead me to some hidden source
that would slake my thirst or satisfy my hunger.
And indeed you kept promising strange things
like water that would become a fountain *within*
springing up to provide eternal life
and a bread that remains forever,
both of which were somehow you, as when you said,
"I myself am living bread,
bread that is flesh."
Or, "Whoever drinks the water I am
will never be thirsty."
What I did not realize
as you spoke so solemnly, placidly,
was that the bread and water

would have to be wrested from you
by a violence I presumed was one of the spirits
you had swept from my house.

You inhabit what we are willing to take by storm,
but I did not know that then.
I did not dream there could be so much violence
in your comings and goings,
even though you said as much when I could not hear.
And it is not a violence done to ourselves or others,
but the violence attendant upon those partings
your presence precipitates.
It is the violence needed
to seize your bloodstained hand,
to embrace your stinking flesh,
to raise you
from the gutters and ditches where you've fallen.
It is the violence of seeing you where you really are,
so that what we take by storm outside
becomes the dwelling place of the inside world
we thought was only a void and empty house
within the lonely heart.

Like bread and wine
you are not just there for the taking
but emerge from ground wheat baking,
crushed grapes fermenting.
It is in the violence of our slow and smokeless burning
and of our sweeteners turning sour
that we find you in the emptied house we fled,
in search of the house we abandoned
lest we be at home when the seven spirits return
to find us sitting there alone.

14.

It is hard for me to say what I am trying to say,
but the violence of loving is the only way I know you,
the giving and the giving up
that wrenches something deep inside
and brings to the surface
what I thought could only come as a gift
from heaven or somewhere else outside the heart.
Everything has an inside and an outside,
and the inside pushes out when the outside pushes in,
and the pushing is violent
and its force stems from the heart inspirited.
That, I suppose, is the Gospel I would write
had I the courage of the others,
their certainty and zeal,
and did I not fear the edge
my words would carry with them,
the edge perhaps of the violence
I am trying ineptly to describe.

But, of course, I needn't talk to you of violence.
You who experienced the pull of inner and outer
from the very beginning
when you pitched your tent in your mother's womb
and, wondering where your Father was,
began to grow outward into a light
which became instead a darkness
that did not master the light you had already become
in the darkness of Mary's womb.
You had become inside
what you were seemingly pushing toward outside;
you lit up the stable
and enkindled the straw where you lay.

And the same thing happened
when you picked up your tent again
to be carried into the darkness of Egypt,
a violent, tortured way of finally going to Nazareth,
which as a town was another kind of darkness
from which no one expected a great light to shine.
And all of these first journeys were mere preludes
to the great journey to Jerusalem
and the violent death which awaited you there
where everyone expected only light and life.

Jerusalem,
before whose gates
all our journeys will end.
Outside the gates
of this city we have yearned to enter all our lives,
we will be destroyed
and the place of our going down
will be where we rise
by a power greater than that movement of the human heart
which began the journey.

The mind thought the end would be recognizable
in the taste of victory.
Instead, the failure to arrive
and the taste of defeat at the city's gates
is what we experience.
And we cry out,
"God, our God, why have you forsaken us?"
Then at the very moment
we begin to descend into the earth,
we begin to break through
to the other side of the earth
where we stand rubbing our eyes,

blinded by the light
that greets us at the other end
of that dark passage.

I know this is true
because the Father, who raised you up,
also raised us up in you.
The Father handed over all creation to you
when they raised against the sky
the tree that held your pierced flesh,
whose blood pouring out
yeasted the earth with rising.
You took everything with you when you left,
everything that is only waiting to follow in its turn
you whose feet ascending we cling to.

15.

Like the cranes I watched as a boy,
those cranes who freed me from my little town of Cana
when I imagined myself flying with them,
you freed us from smallness,
from our petty, self-absorbed worlds.
And that is what healed us,
and is what you taught us about healing.
It moves us beyond the narrow, personal circle
of pain and suffering and frustration,
to the world beyond and toward our part
in expanding that world for others.

Somehow you conveyed to us,

and to anyone who would listen,
the liberating power of self-forgetfulness,
by a life whose focus is on God and others.
We were not to work directly at forgetting ourselves,
but on building the Kingdom.
And if that did indeed become our focus,
we forgot that we were broken or cowardly or sick.

In seeking first the Kingdom of God and his justice
we possessed our lives in a way we did not think possible.
We felt whole though we did not dwell on it or work on it.
Instead of trying to repair our shattered selves
by looking inward, we reached outward,
and our whole being came together
and followed the movement of our open,
outstretched hands.

In that sense the journey to Jerusalem
was your own journey of healing.
Everything had been closing in for months;
and as the circle of your enemies tightened around you,
you broke through the ring
and, putting your own peril aside,
moved toward the violent God who dwells in Jerusalem.
"It is unthinkable," you said,
"for a prophet to meet his death anywhere but Jerusalem."

I remember how you had shocked us
about six months before.
You said you were going to appear in Jerusalem
for the Feast of Tabernacles,
not publicly, but secretly
in order to observe the temper of your enemies.
I knew, however, that you wouldn't be able to resist.

And sure enough, before the festival was over,
there you were speaking to the crowds in the Temple.
And from that moment on
you knew what would happen on that final Passover journey
you had already planned for six months from then.
You knew the terrible truth
of how your mission would be consummated.
The years of doubt were over.

16.

And so we left Transjordan
and crossed over to the west bank.
We stopped at Jericho and Bethany
between the Jordan's banks and Jerusalem
and made our way along the winding, dusty road
to the City of God.

At the edge of the suburbs of Jerusalem
you embraced who you really are.
You mounted a donkey for the final journey into the Kingdom.
At the time I thought you were doing the humble thing,
a symbolic enactment of your own teaching.
But now I see that your riding on the foal of an ass was more.
And it was not just for the benefit of the crowds.
It was for you, as well.

You needed to become at last
who you had realized you were
when you visited Jerusalem six months before:
a poor man on a donkey.

The carcasses of the swift steeds of Yahweh
lay strewn about the gates of the city,
for he himself, as Zechariah foretold,
had banished "chariots from Ephraim
and war-horses from Jerusalem."

And now his Son was coming,
"his cause won, his victory gained,
humbled and mounted on an ass,
on a foal, the young of a she-ass."
You were not enacting something for others;
you were mounting your own destiny.

But as I watched you,
suddenly *you* were the donkey,
the young *foal* of Mary.
You were God become beast of burden,
and the man riding the donkey was me,
was every one of us.

The crowds, of course, misunderstood
and saluted the rider
instead of the humble God
who bore us into his own city.

17.

Once it became clear to you
that the end of the journey was your own death
you began talking to that soul within your soul,
trying to make friends

with the strange, inarticulate voice
that would rise to your mouth at times
and jumble your words with a fear or anger
that surprised you and terrified you.

It seemed to me that the closer we got to Jerusalem,
the more you would talk to us
as if you were talking to someone inside yourself
whom you were trying to console or subdue
so that you could meet your attackers in peace.
The battle you were waging within
seemed to come to a head that day
when the messenger burst into the room and announced
that your friend Lazarus was ill.
Your response seemed to me to be to yourself
rather than to us:
"This illness will not end in death;
it has come for the glory of God,
to bring glory to the Son of God."

No one had said anything about death,
so it must have been on your mind
that you jumped in so quickly
to head off thinking
even about its possibility.
Of course, I am looking back, second-guessing,
but even at that time I sensed that your first response
to the news of Lazarus's illness
was directed to something beyond that situation.
The way you stumbled over your words
and the quickness of your reaction
tells me now
that you were rehearsing your response
to your own death.

And my hunch was reinforced by Thomas's strange remark
when you said we were leaving immediately to visit Lazarus:
"Let's go, then, so we may die with him."
Again it was death that was mentioned,
as if that was what was really on everyone's mind,
what we kept trying to brush aside
as foolishness or mere anxiety.
And when we arrived at Bethany,
it was in fact death that greeted us.

People were milling about the house
and Martha was running out to meet us,
crying out through her tears,
"If you had been here, sir,
my brother would not have died."

Sir?
The formality almost made me laugh.
Martha, Martha, so much like me,
her sarcasm always there,
never missing a chance to make someone feel guilty,
but always catching herself immediately,
lest she lose the opportunity
to manipulate even you:
"Even now I know that whatever you ask of God,
God will grant you."
The implied criticism of "even now"
brought a smile to your face despite your sorrow and pain.

But when you answered
(and you waited long enough
for Martha to get everyone's attention
and be the center of things)
your words came out flat, matter-of-factly:
"Your brother will live again."
The tone and manner of your response
provoked a further sarcasm from Martha,
who wanted those around to hear something that would show
how very special she and her family were in your eyes.
"I *know* that he will rise again
at the resurrection on the last day."

And then it was that your whole manner changed.
You seemed to be speaking from far away

those words that fell upon our hearts
more bittersweetly than anything you had ever said.
Your eyes—in fact, your whole countenance—
seemed turned inward as you said almost inaudibly,
"I am the resurrection and I am the life.
If you have faith in me,
even though you die,
you shall come to life;
and no one who is alive and has faith
shall ever die."

The silence was almost tangible
as your words began to register
on face after face in the crowd.
There was an air of embarrassment
as we realized
that you were just realizing something yourself.
It was as if we were being let in
on a private conversation
between you and someone else,
and we shouldn't have heard
because the emotion of the moment was forcing you
to utter aloud a profound recognition
of something you knew
but did not know you knew
until that very moment.

And you said almost in a daze,
our faces having blurred for you,
"Do you believe this?"
The voice I heard seemed to be coming from the tomb
where you lay with Lazarus, inside Lazarus,
having somehow become Lazarus.
And though you seemed dead,

you were really alive,
waiting for yourself
to summon yourself from the tomb.

Then even Martha transcended herself
and said without sarcasm
in a voice behind the voice she normally used,
"I now believe that you are the Messiah,
the Son of God who was to come into the world."
And she ran off to get Mary,
who she realized was better suited
for the kind of thing
that Martha was afraid
she might have precipitated.
She wanted out of this kind of seriousness,
and so she said to Mary, her usual voice returning,
"The Master is here; he is asking for *you*."
You weren't, of course,
but now Martha could busy herself
with the kinds of things she could manage and understand.
And Mary came immediately
to the place outside the village
where we were all still standing,
staring at you
who seemed bound by invisible linen bands,
staring at the realization
that you were alive and breathing
and lying in a tomb.

And Mary ran up and fell at your feet saying,
"O sir, if you had only been here,
my brother would not have died."
Then you suddenly came back to us,
sighed heavily and said

through your own incipient tears,
"Where have you laid him?"
I expected you to say, "Where have you laid *me*?"
so painfully did you seem to be trying to get out
of the dark earth that was suffocating you
and me and all of us who had become a part
of whatever it was you were struggling with.

Almost simultaneously those around you burst out,
"Come and see!"
and you broke down and cried,
as Mary took your arm
and led you, staggering, to the tomb.

18.

And again you sighed,
but it seemed this time a sigh of relief,
as if this moment were the clarification
of everything that had troubled you.
I thought of what had happened the past three years
and how you would lie down on the cold earth at night,
worn out, frustrated that so few had heard,
feeling a failure,
frightened at where your own words and actions
were leading you and your followers.

You seemed almost paralyzed at times
by the responsibility that had somehow become yours
without your even noticing
how it was growing like a cancer within you:

There was no way you could be responsible for everyone,
that you could be the center of their hopes,
their faith in Yahweh.

But, from the moment you stood at the tomb of Lazarus,
your attitude began to change.
It was here that your real responsibility became clear.
You were to descend into the womb of the earth
and listen to the Father's command,
"Take away the stone. Lazarus, come forth!"
You saw your own face wrapped in a cloth,
your hands and feet swathed in linen bands,
and it was to the Father you spoke when you said,
"Loose him; let him go,"
because you knew that his rising
was what your own approaching death was all about.

In Lazarus were you and everyone else who would rise
if you could seed the earth
with your own body descending.
Somehow you knew it would happen,
that this action at Bethany
was your real responsibility,
the only word and act of your life
that would matter in the end.
And so you shouted with tears of joy,
"Father, I thank you; you have heard me.
I knew already that you always hear me,
but I spoke for the sake of the people standing round,
that they might believe that you *did* send me."

I felt, when you spoke those pretentious words,
that what you claimed to "know"
about the Father always hearing you,
was only now registering in your heart.
And further, when you said the words,
you stumbled at the end, stammering
"that *You* might believe,"
and then correcting yourself to
"that *they* might believe that you did send me."
You seemed to have realized something new:
that the Father would know you were his Son
if you surrendered yourself
to lie like Lazarus in the earth,
waiting for him to lift you up,
drawing all things to you.

My own head began to pound
and I thought I would faint
with the recognition of the fate
that awaited us who followed you.

We were being prepared
for the same sending forth from you
that you were being prepared for by the Father.
The word we spoke would be authenticated
by our seeding the earth with our lives, too.

19.

How quiet this lake is now.
All creatures inside and outside the mind hide,
fleeing as the sun begins to rise.
High in the blue sky above me,
it blinds me with the remembrance
that you were the sun of God, Son of God,
but you did not live among us as a god.
Rather, like a prophet,
your whole life hung upon a past promise
whose fulfillment was yet to be seen
in the day-to-day unfolding of your destiny.
You came, not on your own initiative,
but were sent
to do the will of One who sent you.
And that will was revealed to you
only in the gradual unfolding
of your life as a man.

Those who did not realize
the prophetic nature of what you were about
did not realize either
why you kept straining toward your own end
in order to discover who you were in your origins,

to discover what Isaiah meant when he said,

> ...my servant, whom I have chosen,
> my beloved, on whom my favor rests;
> I will put my spirit upon him,
> and he will proclaim judgment among the nations.
> He will not strive, he will not shout,
> nor will his voice be heard in the streets.
> He will not snap off the broken reed,
> nor snuff out the smoldering wick,
> until he leads justice on to victory.
> In him the nations shall place their hope.

I am not the poet,
the visionary, your beloved John is.
But I sat beneath the trees of my youth
long enough to learn how to think,
to imagine you playing in a carob tree
as a boy, and still see you Isaiah's servant as well.
And had I the eloquence of John,
the Good News I would proclaim
to those who, like me, sit and think and wonder,
is this: Your great poverty was in the struggle
of the man-Jesus (who did not know who he was)
with the God-Jesus (who did).
These were the polarities of who you were,
and your whole life long you were bringing together
this God and this man within you.
In the end that inner reconciliation
also brought together God and all creation
which you also contained in your person.

All during your life
the God kept summoning you to become

that which the man knew only in promise,
only insofar as it was gradually revealed to him.
In you the Messiah became
not a king but a servant,
as the man-Jesus was servant to the God-Jesus.

The whole relationship of God and his people
was summed up and made real for us
in the struggle of the Word to become a man:
The man listened,
the man obeyed,
the man gradually became the Word he was living.
He was lifted up from death by obedience
to the very Word he had been obedient to in life;
he and the Word rose from the tomb
a new man, the Son of Man.
He became Messiah
by becoming servant to his own Word.

Everything you were to become,
the Word's messenger spoke to your mother:
"The power of the Most High
will cast its shadow upon you."
You became the shadow of the power of God,
the underside, the powerlessness that, like a shadow,
depends wholly on something other for its existence.
But the other was also you,
that Godhead whom the man kept discovering in himself
by listening to and doing what it said,
until on Calvary the sun was darkened
and there was no more shadow
and you became the radiance
which, when lifted up, draws all things to itself
as to the source of life and light.

The shadow we cast looking upon you
(a new sun coming upon the clouds of heaven)
is the underside of who we are;
and the shadow becomes one with us
only in our surrender to the darkening
of the sun on our own cross,
on our own lonely hill, head bent,
our arms outstretched as if in flight
toward the fading, shortening shadow
on the earth.

20.

How deep was the gloom of that day
as we turned away from Calvary
and walked repentantly toward Jerusalem
and the temple whose veil our supposed idolatry had ripped
and torn from top to bottom.
And all, we know now,
because we had indeed failed to hear what the words,
the parables were saying:
that you were becoming the words
as the Word had first become a man;
you were the parable.

And we did not see,
as your words grew fewer and far between,
that we were acting out the words you had spoken
and that soon there would be no more words
and no more need for words
because you would yourself become the final utterance,

the final revelation of God:
God forsaking himself that we might live—
"My God, my God, why have you forsaken me?"

God forsaking his own divinity
is the final realized parable;
that is the secret you revealed
from the moment you met Satan in the desert
through the miracles you did not perform,
to the nation you did not save politically,
to the power you did not use,
to the avenging angels you refused upon the cross,
to the final abdication of Godhead
when you failed to save your own life.

It was no joke.
It was not cruel Yahweh laughing.
It was Yahweh's final identification with his people.
From the moment of his dying on Calvary,
He would no longer speak from above
but from within his creation.
And if we were to hear his Word
we must henceforth listen to ourselves speaking:
We became the revelation of God from within his own people.
We would meet him
while we were walking the road to Emmaus,
and he would reveal himself in the breaking of bread,
the drinking of wine around a table become altar
by our gathering there to remember his final revelation,
Jesus Christ.

You, Lord God, had become the neighbor we met on the road
or the stranger become neighbor because of you.
And all the sadness of that afternoon on Calvary

that forced us to turn to one another for comfort and support
was really the finger of God pointing from the cross
to where he would dwell from then on:
among us.

N O O N

1.

A stooped woman is walking the beach below my tree,
her basket of fish doubling her over with its weight.
She turns almost imperceptibly to where I am sitting.
She eyes me cautiously and walks on, quickly,
her weighted back reminding me of that other woman,
your mother.

Almost as young as you, how old she looked,
how bent, as she held your dead body in her arms
a symbol of the sorrow of all parting.
What can I say now that she is here without you?

Every time I see her and count more gray hairs,
more wrinkles than before,
I wonder who she is,
this fiftyish woman
whose presence plagues us with memories of you.
She reminds me of something feminine in myself,
something I used to fear,
another "I" crying to be heard,
to be placated by something I had to give but would not.
Something vestigial perhaps,
an ending or a prefix to a noun.

Lately, she has begun to walk through my dreams
as if she belongs there,
or is she in fact inside me
because that is where she really dwells, this Mary,
this mother whose presence haunts me
more than your absence,
you who are her only son?
Or are you?

Did I not see my own reflection in your eyes
that day you called me
and every day we walked together?
And yet I never thought
you were the brother I never had,
nor do I now.
Nor is she my mother.
It is something other.

She is somehow me
(I can't believe what I'm saying),
the me you left behind when you ascended to the Father,
taking part of me with you
on the soles of your feet,
the me who is the empty womb you broke through,
rising from death.

Salvation is no longer just an entering in,
but a coming out, as well.
The walls of Jerusalem, the walls of a tomb,
are meaningless now that you have died
and risen beyond them.
From the bosom of your Father
you entered the womb of Mary
in order to come out into the world outside.
In her the walled city took on flesh,
became human, woman;
and all need of mortar and stone became superfluous.
In Mary and through her
all salvation began to happen inside out,
and God kept breaking out
of what was supposed to contain him:
the womb, the tent, the Temple, the city,
even the earth where he lay buried under our sins.
Whatever you entered
became pregnant with your birth
rather than a permanent throne for residing.

All creation is for birthing
rather than enthroning God-become-flesh.
Perhaps that is why your mother moves me so:
In her presence
something in me struggles to conceive.

The mystery of it all staggers me.
Perhaps that is your mother Mary's fascination
for me.
You inhabit her still
and are born again and again through her.
Even now she is like a walking pregnancy,
full of grace, filled with you,

and to touch her
is to touch the mystery
of the enfleshment of God.

I struggle to say it and cannot.
I can only report the ringing in my ears
when she speaks to us.
God is born of woman
is all I can say.
It is so obvious
as to sound like a cliché already;
but it is not grasped,
I am sure,
because we keep looking for you, Jesus,
up there in the heavens.

We keep looking for you in all the wrong places.
(Perhaps I should not even have come here to this lake!)
We remain in Jerusalem,
and you are on the road,
or you are eating supper in some house in Emmaus.

I am spending more time with your mother.
She seems to know where you are.
Or perhaps she carries you to where you should be:
among the poor, the outcast,
the rejected and despised.
She spends little time with us,
as you know,
I'm sure.

2.

And so my memories of you and those around you
are human ones
that only make your divinity more resplendent
for all its human skin.
And Mary leaps into the mind again and again
with all the freshness and color of the mystical bride,
"the eyes behind her veil like doves,
her hair like a flock of goats
streaming down Mount Gilead."

She is all of that and none of that,
because your mother,
when it all started happening,
was merely a poor girl of Nazareth
living the simple, nondescript existence of the poor.
Then there was the angel
and your birth
and the wise men from the East,
the flight into and return from Egypt,
presenting you,
then finding you in the Temple,
and the marriage in Cana, my village,
and the cross and the resurrection.
Those were the extraordinary events,
the events that raised her high above the ordinary.

But it is how she lived
and what she did from day to day that matters,
and it all transpires inside the earthen walls of her home.
She is the divinization of the domestic,
as you are the humanization of the Godhead.

She it was who spoke most truly of you,
she it was who sat quietly
in the shadow of the Temple and spoke with me
and understood my troubled heart
and calmed me with what she remembered
and how she remembered it:

He rode lightly in my womb like a dream
    of clouds floating me above the earth
And I would place my hand on my belly
    and I would tremble
At who this would be
    growing within me, apart from me.

And Joseph, the tender, miraculous man,
    would place his warm fingertips on the moving Life
And look into my eyes and feel his estrangement
    from what had entered me without him and try
To comfort me when he wanted only to cry.
    And we would sit for hours near the doorway
Where the Sabbath sun made a rectangular box

And plan what we would do when this child,
    whose name we already knew was Jesus,
Would crawl into the sun-box and reach for the light
    with his tiny hand and we would know he was
The Son of God and wonder what he knew—or would he
    talk and not be speechless like other children?

And how we cried for joy when he was born
    and did not talk but lay there like a baby and was.
We knew then we need only be like other people until the day
    when the child became aware of what we already knew.

Though he was divine, the Godhead in that tiny body
    revealed itself to him as the Torah reveals itself to a rabbi—
Line by line and only when it could be absorbed
    and understood by the student, though this disciple
Knew more but would not know he knew more until
    the dialogue began and the rush of love between
Father and Son took him the way it had taken me
    in his conception.

She leaned back against the Temple wall where we sat—
this woman of fifty or so and I,
who dared to ask and dared as well to listen.
Her feet reached for the spot of sun
that was beginning to inch over the east wall
and she looked at me where I looked on in wonder
at the poetry of her speaking.
She crossed her hands in her lap
and I noticed the small brown spots of age
just beginning to form in a couple of places.

And I wondered if she always talked like this
or if this was one of those special moments for us,
one of those magic moments
when question and answer, speaker and listener
become one
in the spark of encounter that ignites something in the soul
that needs to flame up and burn itself out
that the heart might lie down, tranquil again,
satisfied that its light has shone
before one whose eyes were made to see it.

I dared not speak.
I waited at her feet,
not knowing if the fire was out or not,
not knowing if this was all I would see
of what was kept burning
from all she had stored in her heart like precious fuel.

3.

Though we dared not even think about it,
   we knew we were giving God a home.
And the walls of the house were suddenly mud
   and the floor was dirt and we were poor.
I was pregnant before the seemly time
   and our neighbors knew and ostracized us,
And there was much silence at the table
   when Joseph came in from the shop for supper.
We would try to talk about the pleasantries and he
   always smiled and lifted the cup of wine to his lips
Gratefully, as if for the meal and me and everything
   that remained unspoken between us.

But behind the smile, behind the quiet manner,
   I could see the passion and how he wanted to take me
In his arms and did not know if he dared with the
   Father of my child still fanning the air about us.
And he would rise and return to the shop after supper
   and I could hear the sawing and the wood falling
And the too heavy clomping back and forth
   as he tried to wear himself out pouring his
Frustrated love into the mechanical movement of arm
   and saw, the methodical stacking of even boards.
And he would then come in after he thought
   I was already asleep and fall exhausted onto the bed
Where I lay, eyes closed and weeping for him.

And then there was the danger from without,
   and we with no means of protection, no hiding place
Except in the words we had grown used to hearing,
   words we feared and prayed would not be too hard
In the fulfilling, words that seemed to contradict

the words of the Law, so that I would lower my eyes
And cling to the wall-side of the street when I was
    out shopping and a rabbi passed by,
Words like those that once startled us in sleep and drove us
    from our home onto the desert road to Egypt.

And here she lay back and sighed as if the memory were too much,
the danger and pain still alarmingly real, even now,
and yet wanting to try and tell it this time,
to exorcise what she never told Joseph or the child
whose safety was responsible for that terrible journey
that was the fulfillment of another prophecy
she would have been happy to leave unfulfilled.

    How I began to resent the Law and the prophets.
        They loomed like monsters in my mind and devoured
    Us for their own unalterable purposes. Always
        the Law and the prophets, as if our whole existence were
    Only that they might be justified in my son,
        as if he had been born only to make all those
    Unrealized promises come true once and for all, to silence
        the scribes and Pharisees whose lives were words.
    Words, and the only way to satisfy them was to
        give them a walking, talking man whose every
    Gesture reminded them of a passage in some
        obscure text so they could beam with discovery.

    Only it did not work that way. The more the words
        came true, the more they felt the young man was only
    Using the words to enhance his own ruthless ambition
        to become Messiah and cause dissension and overthrow
    The very Law he claimed to be fulfilling and bring bloodshed
        upon his people as the Roman heel crushed
    Into the ground the final remnant of our freedom.

75

And he grew up before my eyes, my very God's Son,
   whose own Law lurked in the shadows about the house,
Like his mortal enemy. And I watched in wonder.
   I looked at him and knew who his Father was
And wondered if the boy would ask, and when.
   And I began to dread the day he would leave us
In search of his real Father, that inevitable day
   that would fulfill the final words and rid us forever
Of the unreasonable demands of the Law become God.
   He would become the Law that thought it was destroying him.

But first he had to pass through
those awkward years when a boy tries
To become a man.

And she smiled tenderly
for the first time since her canticle began.

4.

I was about to continue my narrative
when the branches of this tree swayed gently
and I suddenly realized that
the sharp edge is gone from my words;
and I cannot remember when or where it disappeared,
except that the more defined you become in my remembering,
the closer you seem to be
and the more divine is your presence.
I no longer experience the bitterness of your leaving
or feel that skeptical specter rising inside me.
I only want you to be present to me
and help me, as I remember,
to make you present in the words I utter falteringly.
Only you can make my dead words live,
only your spirit rekindles the smoldering fire within them.
My own poor words are becoming the Word.

But there she is again,
her eyes shining with what she is telling me
of how it was with her.

How is it this strange boy, who had clung

so long to my dress and held my hand to market
And back and through the narrow streets to synagogue,
    should now become a man like other boys?
I had thought that with him it would be different,
    that some angel would come in the night
And wing him away while we slept.
    And then he would return one day and stand
In the door fully a man, his eyes deep with prophecy,
    his face still shining from where he had been.

But here he was instead, an awkward boy, his voice
    deepening, a small line of hair sprouting above
His lip, looking at his young mother, wondering if he
    dare ask her what was happening to him.
And I wanting to embrace him and reassure him
    but turning instead to Joseph who saw as well
And took the boy by the hand and walked with him.

They returned, I remember, very late, and
    the boy entered too solemnly, I thought, and carefully
As if carrying the burden of a great new knowledge
    that endeared him to me even more and I smiled
As he came to me formally, almost humorously,
    and kissed me protectively upon the forehead.
Joseph winked from where he stood smiling
    at the open door, and I suddenly felt chilled
And saw something frightening flit by the door,
    something that would return for the boy.

And I reached out and drew my son to myself,
    and he started at the fear I could not hide
And thought it was because he was beginning
    to grow away from me, and he held me close
And remembered he was still only a boy.

I could not believe the candor with which she was speaking
and saw that she was tiring
and did not want to remember the rest:
the years of your leaving and Joseph's dying,
the years of rumor and whispered threats upon your life
that became more and more frequent and less quiet
until they were saying openly and boldly
that you were dangerous and must be silenced,
that you blasphemed Yahweh,
that you would surely die
if you continued the madness of your ways.
But she did in fact continue, her head heavy with memories.

And it did return, the thing in the night,
    and took him away,
But by that time I was almost relieved.
    At last he had found himself
This boy trying to become a man even
    to his thirtieth year.
All his companions were long since
    married with children about the house
And Jesus still came dreamily in from the shop
    and sat down for supper staring vacantly at us
As if expecting some reprimand for being there
    instead of wherever he was supposed to be.
He always seemed so lost, like an abandoned child
    waiting hopelessly for someone to come for him.

And then John began to preach beyond the Jordan
    and Jesus' footsteps began to lighten about the house
And a light came into his eyes as if someone was finally
    saying something he was interested in.
He asked people about John every chance he got,
    and one day he went to see him and he did not return.

79

And that night I saw the dark thing at the window
as I lay sleepless in the empty house.

And, of course, you know the rest, Nathanael.

That was all she ever told me, but it was enough;
and sometimes I still hear her voice
as I am drifting off to sleep
and I see the pain in her eyes and their joy
when she concluded with,
"And, of course, you know the rest, Nathanael."
She had never called me anything but "the Israelite" before,
and I used to imagine you
telling her about the "true Israelite" you had found
sitting beneath a fig tree just as you used to sit
when you did not know who you were
and were feeling sorry for yourself like Jonah.
And she, of course, would remember
because it did in fact remind her of her son
and all the worry she had for what would become of him
who sat in the shade of trees
instead of cutting wood with Joseph.
True Israelites are worthy of the name.
In them God did indeed strive.

5.

"The thing in the night"
that took you away from your mother
was really what most of us call "death,"
that final frustration
of the destiny we have fashioned for ourselves
and which we dared believe was in our grasp.
When you were thirty years old,
you surrendered to the destiny
mapped out for you from all eternity

by the very divinity who was now emerging
from the depths of your own awareness.

You began to yield to that mysterious self
that used to frighten you as a boy,
that voice that held you behind in Jerusalem
when you were twelve,
that self you became before the doctors of the Law
as you sat listening to them and asking them questions
you did not know you knew.
You let yourself be led away
from the familiar, comfortable life you had made for yourself
toward the desert
where, as you said to Peter,
"Another shall gird you,
and lead you where you do not want to go."

All journeys of the spirit begin,
as Abraham's did,
with leaving the comfortable,
familiar land of one's youth
and trekking through the desert of powerlessness;
and they all end with words like yours on the cross:
"Father, into your hands I commit my spirit."
And as I sat talking to Mary
in the shadow of the Temple,
I suddenly realized
that your journey
had been a journey from your mother to your Father.
The great and terrible chasm that opened up beneath you
could only be bridged by letting go of your mother's hand
and somehow leaping far enough
toward your Father's outstretched hand
to catch it and not fall into the void.

That is what you meant by faith, isn't it?
The journey from mother to Father
across the void
that letting go of a mother's hand created.
Now I understand
your mother's willingness to let you go
and how she smiled
when she spoke of you not returning
to the house of your youth.

She realized, didn't she,
that you had finally met the angel she met as a young girl
and that you were letting go of her
as she had of her parents, Joachim and Anne;
that your failure to return
meant you had heard your Father's voice
and had accepted your manhood
as she had her womanhood
when she said,
"Behold the handmaid of the Lord;
let it be unto me according to your word"?

And Mary was then at peace because she knew
that in embracing your manhood,
you discovered what she had known from the beginning
and dared not say:
"You are God's beloved Son; in you he is well pleased."

ACT III

D U S K

1.

The black rocks near the shore seem blacker now.
They have become the real stones they are,
instead of the tops of water-castles
they seemed in the morning light.

Stones in the water.
Like the stories of you
that the community is preserving,
they reveal only the tip of all they are.
The stories are the water-stones
of who you were, who you are:
Jesus, Lord,
the man from Nazareth.
And here on this little rise above the lake,
I have been looking at their surfaces,
eyeing them from my vantage point
beneath this fig-laden tree.

Now, with evening coming on,
my memory is somehow submarine,
and I find myself sliding down the rocks' surfaces
into underwater fathoming,
and suddenly there is the young Zachary,
lying nervously awake,
fearing that once again she has failed to conceive—
this strong, patient woman beside him,

And Elizabeth refusing to weep
lest she show him
how deep is her fear
of one more failure.
She has not borne him a child,
and he has not made her fruitful.
They are both on edge
from the guilt of letting each other down,
and so they blame themselves—
which makes Zachary feel she is blaming him
and Elizabeth that he is blaming her.
And the incessant prayers,

the words ascending more like complaints than petitions,
and both of them worrying
that the anger coming through their cries
is preventing Yahweh from hearing,
from answering their prayer.

Then the passing of the years, and old age,
and Zachary's terror on seeing the angel
standing on the right of the altar of incense.
Surely he has come to punish Zachary's anger and doubt
and bitterness toward the fecund God
who has withheld life from Elizabeth's womb so long
that now it is too late
and all their hopes lie dead
inside the woman he hoped to make happy with children
who would hang from the beams of their home
like fat and juicy grapes.
And then this incredible promise of a son—
but even in this answer
all these strange qualifications and stipulations
as if the son were really not theirs but Yahweh's
and he is only using them to beget a prophet
who will be estranged from his parents from birth.
And the angel,
as if anticipating Zachary's thoughts,
saying, "Your heart will thrill with joy
and many will be glad that he was born."

Then, despite his joy,
all the years of false hopes
and almost-pregnancies overtake him
and the words come out in bitterness,
full of doubt and unwonted sarcasm:
"How can I be sure of this?

I am an old man and my wife is well on in years."
(Even here before the angel of the Lord
he cannot call her old and will not.
The hurt has been too great,
and he will protect her name even before the Lord himself.)

He feels himself growing in stature
even in his fear
and the Lord understands
and treats him like the worthy opponent he has become
through the shame of his failure.
And the Lord's messenger seems to stand straighter
and addresses him like a patriarch:
"I am Gabriel; I stand in attendance upon God,
and I have been sent to speak to you
and bring you this good news.
But now listen:
you will lose your power of speech,
and remain silent until the day
when these things happen to you,
because you have not believed me,
though at their proper time
my words will be proved true."

And he tries to respond but cannot
and his heart fills with fear and joy at once.
Finally Yahweh has taken him seriously,
finally he has heard and made him dumb.
Yahweh has heard what he is feeling
and has responded in kind.
He loves the anger of the Lord.
It feels so good to know he has provoked God to action—
even this action, this knotting of his tongue.
And his crazy laughter fills the temple like grunts.

2.

How marvelous the mercy of Yahweh,
how pointed his sense of humor:
Elizabeth to be with child and he, Zachary, struck dumb!
How they will laugh, the old men of the village:
she pregnant beyond the time of bearing and he,
who never shut up,
struck dumb by it all.
Already Zachary can hear the jokes they will make,
for out of the deepest tragedy
and the most profound mystery of our lives
come the jokes, the incongruities
that others find amusing and really are,
when we view them from without.
And even we who experience their mockery
have to laugh at times
when we put ourselves in their place
and see what they see.

These are the kinds of thoughts that rush in
as evening descends
because they seem to me a memory
of something I should not forget
even though I have never witnessed what I remember,
nor do I know what is so significant
about these images and stories that run through my mind.
I could not tell anyone their meaning;
they only remind me of you.

3.

I remember often that winter of snow
that fell in large pails upon the barren hillsides
in whose bowels we were holed up shivering
and laughing against the cold.
You joked about those bowels being as empty as Elizabeth,
the barren hillside not unlike her barren womb.
We were together a lot that winter;
we had you much to ourselves.
I'm sure that you must have instructed us,
but I don't remember what you said
or even that you said much at all.
In fact, you never said or taught much
when we were away from the crowds.
Instead, you joked and you listened.
And that is what I remember most
about that winter
seeding down from heaven,
turning dark and barren hillsides
into bright snow:
how you laughed and how you listened.

So many times in preaching to the people
you seemed rapt in another world,
as if you were listening to your Father tell you what to say.
You were the complete prophet,
speaking for Yahweh
to whom you listened with your whole being,
a man possessed of God,
a man who heard only the voice that he called "Father."

But then during those weeks and months
as we sat about the fire in our caves,

I saw that you listened to us as well,
and to all of creation around and within you.
Your whole manner was that of a listener,
one whose very way of hearing
made the one speaking feel understood at last
and accepted,
and the speaker's words would somehow return from you
ordered and sanctified and healed
by humor and love.
In hearing your response,
something came together inside the person
who dared speak to you from the heart.
As with Elizabeth,
the barren womb we thought we were
began to leap with the child within us.

And you listened to plants and animals,
stones and fish and birds, as well.
And they became more who they were
in your affirming hearing.
You listened to the music of their being
as you listened to the stories of our lives
and the Word of the Father.
And just as your listening had been so perfect
that you became the enfleshment of that Word,
so your hearing us was so whole
that you spoke back to us who we were becoming.

You seemed to grow more divine each day,
as if what you heard from the Father
was taking on flesh in you.
And so real was this growing divinity we all saw in you
that by the time you hung lifeless upon the tree,
we had forgotten that you were also human.

Divinity seemingly absorbed into the human:
That is what my limited vision saw happening in you.
You were totally Jesus of Nazareth,
but the words that came back from you
seemed to have entered a divine dimension
where they found the realities they were naming,
recognized them, and returned to tell us joyful news:
The word was again connected to what it named.
And that is what healed us.
That is what heals anyone, then and now and forever:
Someone listening with the hopeful ear of God—
Only *that* connects what has been severed,
only *that* brings together
the shattered shards of the self.

4.

That winter,
with the stems of desert flowers
cracking in the cold wind,
their petals long gone
from the place of their making,
the barrenness of Elizabeth
seemed to be everywhere.
Then, especially,
we would hear those words of love you gave us,
those words to find you by.

We would wake up cold and shivering,
wanting only someone next to us,
warm skin insulating us

from the sterile grip of cold,
and "Seek first the Kingdom of Heaven"
the *last* thing on our minds.
We would only want to give it all up
for a fruitful human embrace,
but instead we'd try once more
the power of your word upon the tongue
and, opening our eyes and mouths,
we would sigh, trying a prayer:
"We scatter seed on the land;
we go to bed at night and get up in the morning,
and the seed sprouts and grows—
how, we don't know.
Oh, teach us to know, if nothing else,
that our barren lives
are at least scattering seed on the land!"

It is not winter here now,
but the desert grows dark and cold,
evening time that makes me
wonder what my life has become
because of you, and what it is that is missing
that makes your words ring hollow
in this dry night wind,
the capricious wind "that blows where it wills;
you hear the sound of it,
but you do not know where it is going."
And I remember how many times you said
that we do not know or would not know,
but that "everything is possible
to one who has faith."

I sink deep down inside myself again,
reaching for your hand,

your words sustaining me like air
in that deep dive to do battle
with the beast who stalks my heart,
demanding that I at least acknowledge his presence.
I cannot deny him;
I can only meet him
surrounded by the armor of your words.

I close my eyes and stammer illogically,
"I have faith, help my faithlessness."
And I know what I must do
before your words will enable me
to live through another day in praise,
instead of dread.
I stand before the enemy/friend
who rises naked
from the dark, frozen womb of myself,
and I realize that he is the first one
you were thinking of when you said,
"If, when you are bringing your gift to the altar,
you suddenly remember
that someone has a grievance against you,
leave your gift where it is before the altar.
First go and make your peace with that person,
and only then come and offer your gift."

And I am forced again to consider
how I have not spun the web that holds me
nor am I myself the thread of its securing.
I am only he who hangs there in space,
either celebrating my free and glorious floating
or fretting about what might unfasten me
and hurl me to the ground.

The beast I face anew each evening
is that fretting, that fear.
And only wrapped in the light of your words
can I face him down
to celebrate another day
of flowing with the breath of God's mouth,
of floating in the insubstantial air of faith.

We begin, always, with the enemy within.
That is why your words of love
are so difficult for me:
They summon me
to begin each day with this inner embrace,
even before I rise from my bed.
They demand that cold journey
through the night
to face again what I do not like to look at,
what I can only face
by summoning your words to sustain me,
by daring to believe that mere words are effective
if I ply their power by doing what they say,
if I, in fact, begin to live the words
that seem only to exist in memory,
altered perhaps in remembering,
altered to fit my need for them.

And I am back again to belief:
Each day is an act of faith in your word,
each night an act of trust
that you will be faithful to what you promised,
that with your words around me,
"I am not alone, because the Father is with me."

Then your words begin to untangle
and become like a strong and intricate web
securing me in space
though it hangs on a single, delicate thread
of faith.

5.

That first winter was our apprenticeship;
that is when we began to understand
the kind of love you had been preaching
because each of us experienced it,
received it from you.
We found in you and in the family you gathered together
an intimacy that had previously been denied us,
even those among us who were married
and had families already.
How is it that we who longed
for the soothing words and soft touch
of another human being
found, in the rough touch of life you gave us
and in the hard words we were to live by,
a closeness to Yahweh and ourselves and others
that kept us with you
despite all the other seeming absurdities,
like walking the cold roads homeless
toward a Kingdom that kept dissolving before us
like mirages in the Judean desert?

I realize now that it was that intimacy, that communion
which lay behind each person's willingness to follow you.
From the onset, when you summoned us,
usually with a perfunctory,
"Follow me,"
it was the embrace of eyes accepting,
approving everything we were,
that drew us as to a mirror that transformed us
into the image we wanted to see reflected there
instead of the image we thought we saw but did not like.

Always, behind the carefully fitted masks we wore,
were the faces we were afraid to try out on others,
the faces we wanted someone to hold and kiss
and see as beautiful.
Faces that were more than faces.

Faces that were really our whole naked selves,
vulnerable, afraid.
Faces that believed they were unlovable,
as they tried so desperately
to pretend and prove they were lovable
by all those insincerities we employ
to ingratiate ourselves to others.

And then you came into our lives,
and we no longer saw what was imperfect within us.
Like Elizabeth we no longer felt barren,
like Zachary, no longer old.
We saw only the love in your eyes,
and you became more important than what was
superficially reflected from all the mirrors
people held up to us.
We looked into your eyes
and the mirror there was not a surface
but more like a reflecting pool
that drew us inside
where everything,
including our own images,
was changed by the gentle pull of your love
which we experienced as a drawing-in
rather than something you gave us
or clothed us with.
Love, we learned from you,
is first a total drawing-in of the other,
a kind of feminine movement,
rather than the phallic thrust
we had thought it to be.
Only one who is totally received
can accept the alms, the cloak, the healing
that reaches out to do for and unto others.

Your eyes were the color of the sea and full of light
and we fell into them as into the waters of the firmament.
And we learned to open our own eyes
to receive whatever we saw,
even I who censored and analyzed everything
that came into my range of seeing, of vision.
Yes, perhaps *vision* is the better word
for how you taught us to see by drawing in.
Seeing, after all, was so often associated with judgment,
with looking for!
"Why do you look at the speck of sawdust
in another's eye,
with never a thought
for the great plank in your own?"

But vision was different.
It looked at a man
covered with wounds and spittle,
a crown of thorns on his head,
and saw "the Son of Man coming in the clouds
with great power and glory."
It looked at a crippled woman being healed on the Sabbath
and saw "how Satan fell like lightning, out of the sky."
It watched a rich person refusing to look into your eyes
and saw a wounded camel
trying to squeeze through the eye of a needle,
and it wept for what refused to enter the open eyes of love.
The vision, then, was not so much what was seen,
but what was received and embraced.
I see only what I bring inside and love.
It is as simple as that.
That kind of love is what you gave us
and why we followed you,
and that kind of love is why

we continue to grow in numbers
despite all our darkness,
despite the fact that we are by and large
who we were all along
before we met you, Lord Jesus.
In fact, it is really not *despite*
but *because* you enabled us
to be the face we were hiding,
that we continue to multiply.
Communion is eyes become pools
instead of mirrors reflecting from harsh surfaces
only the appearance of things.

ACT IV

N I G H T

1.

There are no fires burning by the sea this evening.
There is only my heart burning as I sit by this lake,
a solitary soul searching the shore for other souls
emerging from the evening mist.
From time to time someone does,
but at a distance,

and my solitude is undisturbed,
my monologue with you uninterrupted.
These moments, inside,
days and nights by the sea,
prepare a place in me
for moving inland when morning comes
and the sun burns off the fog,
and I face again the daily search for you
in the lives who pass by
the indifferent shore of my praying.

Soon I will leave you by the remembered sea
where I have seen you cooking fish
for me to eat at nightfall.
And I will leave and return
to find you there, or not,
depending on whom I bring with me.

You, Lord of the sea,
Lord by the sea,
you are the God of the border
between land and water,
between the sky and the land and the sea.
And your small human fire
lights the place where all the elements meet
in the human God who waits for us
to come from the sea or the land
to sit by the fire and eat the fish you cook,
the fish you are become.
And we lay all our daily selves upon the fire
to be consumed by all who eat with you,
by all whose food is the human God
who sits and waits
where earth and water endlessly embrace,

warming the air with their fire.

Mist touches me as I talk with you,
a dense cover from which no man or woman,
no bird or animal has emerged,
an insulating fog
keeping you here a little longer.
A time for dreaming.

I close my eyes,
and there is Peter working furiously with his nets
lest he lose a minute of fishing
should the fog lift and it be a clear night.
And John is there hoping the fog will stay,
and all we other apostles and followers
are somewhere in between.

But whether I go or stay, come night,
it is you who holds me or sends me,
keeps me by the shore or draws me back
to the small fire and the fish.
All movement to and from
revolves about this place by the sea.
The center is you
cooking fish by the Sea of Galilee
whose water caresses the shore of my human heart.

2.

I look up and
the moon is a small wafer in the sky

above my right shoulder.
There is so little time now
before I return to the world outside
and leave you where you found me
by the ashes of the fire
where I began my journey.
Now there is no safeness of sun,
and darkness brings me
to my knees
as it has every night
since your leaving.
In my grief, I cannot seem
to keep my thoughts from turning
to your suffering and death,
the flames rising higher,
consuming the fish,
leaving only the ashes
that you fanned into flame again
as you rose from their cold,
extinguished center.

And again it is your mother I turn to.
Knowing that you would die very soon,
what did she do,
this Mary, the woman whose face haunts me
in my own night of grief?
I see her as I left her,
sitting there upon the ground,
the Temple weighing down her shoulders,
and she like a bundle of discarded clothes
thrown against the walls, the foundations of Israel.
What did she do when she knew
you would die,
you, her lovely son?

How did she get over losing you,
and how can I?

I ask that question many times, Lord Jesus,
especially when I realize how helpless we are
to stave off death
and someone close to us is dying
and we are supposed to have a faith
that moves mountains
because we are your disciples.
Discipleship does not seem to make it any easier,
except that I do have you to call upon,
and vent my anger on, and cry to in my sorrow.

I think of your mother watching you die,
and you become every human pair.
You become every loved one who has died
and she the one who is helpless, watching it all happen,
she believing only that she too will die
of worry and then of grief.

Confronted with death,
we want to kill whatever insults us
with the deception that this corpse before us
is really alive in some other world.
Was it in fact your promise to rise again in three days
that made us kill you?
Who knows?
And surely it made no difference to your mother
what the reason was.
She only knew you were moving headlong into death;
she saw you dying from living too intensely.
And there was nothing she could do,
except try to remember all that had happened,

especially those portentous events that preceded your birth,
except try to search the Scriptures for some hope
that you would be saved in the nick of time.

And perhaps like me she turned to Isaiah,
who had spoken so glowingly of your birth,
hoping he would reveal the meaning of your death.
Or did she look to you, her son,
for the answer to what would become of us all?
I can't know, of course,
but even if she did and found there an answer,
it did not prevent her
from suffering death vicariously with you
before she arrived at some resolution.

As she stood helplessly
beneath your cross and watched you die,
Mary became every one of us in the face of what is human,
what is mortal and beloved.
She watched her own flesh dying in you.

3.

And so I return to the question I began with.
What did she do, your mother,
when she saw you were going to die
and like us was helpless to prevent it?
What did she do then
she who had said in your conceiving,
"Behold the handmaid of the Lord;
be it done to me according to your will"?

What she cannot change
she brings inside her heart and makes it her will.
And that is what she did
when she knew you were going to die a violent death
like so many of the prophets before you.

Mary knew she could not save you from death
because in some mysterious way
it was death itself that would save you,
and through that very death
she who wanted to save you would herself be saved.
She had heard you say,
"Unless the grain of wheat fall into the ground and die,
it will not live."
And she understood.

Unfortunately, however,
understanding and acceptance do not take away the pain
of watching and waiting
for the inevitable death of someone we love.
It only heightens the pain
because we know what we wish we didn't know.
And we cannot think about it
and grieve over it all the time,
and so we continue the routine of our lives,
our domestic chores,
even our joking and trying to relax
and caring for our health,
as if we are to live forever.

And the days pass and we toss fitfully in bed
and wake to the nightmare of the other's death.
We rise earlier and fall asleep
more from exhaustion than relaxation.

And that perhaps is how it was with her who knew,
before we did,
what cup would be offered you in Gethsemane
and what you would say,
that echo of her own words to the angel so many years before:
"Only not as I will but as you will, Father."

And so Mary becomes who we all are at the core,
mortal beings trying to hold back death
until we can accustom ourselves to its frightening visage
in the slow decay or swift passing of those we love.
She had to reach deep down inside,
where you said the Kingdom is
and try to find there
some way of coping with death,
some strength, some hope beyond the grave,
anything to heal the wide wound of separation.

And what she found,
I like to think,
is your own words to Martha that fateful day
you rose with her brother, Lazarus, from the dead:
"I am the resurrection and I am life;
if you believe in me, even though you die,
you shall come to life;
and no one who has life, and has faith in me
shall ever die."
And she knew that the sword which would pierce her own soul
would be the sword that pierced your side
from which flowed the life
by which we all would live forever.

But then, could she live on words?
Was she, like Abraham and so many holy ones before her,
the kind of person who could live
on the promise of things to be fulfilled?
She had to be,
or she never would have consented
to be your mother in the first place.
And now this waiting for your death
was like waiting for you to be born,
or, at Nazareth all those years,
for you to begin the ministry of dying
by which we were to live.
Who can say which waiting was the hardest for her
and which was more like death?

It is perhaps the waiting itself that is the hardest,
and all the uncertainty and anxiety
over what we will do and how we will respond
to the surprises of Yahweh
that is the real dying.
Surely she had died with you many times before,
as on the flight into Egypt
and when she thought you were irretrievably lost
on that journey to Jerusalem when you were twelve.
Perhaps those and all the other dyings
made it easier for her
to handle your approaching death.

But most probably it did not.
For what we know and what we have already experienced
is never sufficient to remove the sting
when we hold in our arms
the broken body of our own child
who should be holding us in death.

That was the sword in Mary's heart,
and that moment of your lying lifeless in her arms
revealed the deepest pain of the human heart.
And the pain was not diminished
simply because you rose from the grave
three days later.
The future was not yet.
We suffer the present,
and it is not changed to joy
until a future hope becomes the present reality.

So now like Mary we live on the promise
that in you the present pain is not forever.
It changes into joy
when your future becomes our present.
For the future has been transformed
into an eternal present
by your dwelling there with the Father
waiting to be made complete
in our joining you.
We *will* live forever.
But the way there is still death
and that has not changed.
It is the painful sword
that reveals the thoughts of many hearts.

Like Mary we still have to hold death in our lap
and embrace it if we are to live forever.
But knowing that does not make the cold body warmer,
the broken body whole,
the heavy weight light like pious thoughts.
For then it would not be dead
and we would not know how heavy life is
before it takes wings.

ACT V

D A W N

1.

It is morning.
I have finally slept.
A few hours at most,
and then only from exhaustion.
Too much thinking,
too much in the head for my own good.

There is a chill in the air
and there is no sun.
Only clouds hiding
what we call the sky,
that blue eternity above.
Or are the clouds also sky,
and we have made the heavens sky
only when they are blue?

Here beneath the tree of my sleeping,
sweet with scent of fig,
the gray above is all the sky there is,
and it contents me somehow
that I can call it sky
and not wait for the clouds to pass
and the sun to shine and the color blue to reappear.

Suddenly I realize that is how it is with you and me,
Lord Jesus.
I do not wait for you to return
for you to be the risen Lord;
you already have,
behind the gray that hides you from our sight.
Your name is Savior Lord,
no matter what the color of your appearing.
It is who you are
and what you did that make you Lord,
not the radiance of your countenance shining
clear and unmistakable
like sun on a blue and cloudless day.
You are Lord,
in hiding or in revealing
who you are,
as on that evening you sat down to meal again

in the startled home at Emmaus.

You were the risen Lord
even before you revealed yourself at supper,
even as you had walked the road earlier that day,
conversing and asking questions like some stranger
to all the events of your own life.
And they did not recognize you,
those two pilgrims walking the road to find you,
and so they told you about yourself,
"a prophet mighty in deed and word
before God and all the people,
and our chief priests and rulers
delivered him up to be condemned
and crucified him.
But we had hoped
that he was the one to redeem Israel.
Yes, and besides all this,
it is now the third day since this happened.
Moreover, some women of our company amazed us.
They were at the tomb early in the morning
and did not find his body;
and they came back saying
that they had even seen a vision of angels,
who said that he was alive.
Some of those who were with us
went to the tomb,
and found it just as the women had said;
but him they did not see."

And then you opened up for them
the gray sky that was always sky
though they called it clouds;
you began with Moses and the prophets

and opened up in the Scriptures
everything that was really about you
though you lay hidden behind the clouds
we did not know were sky.

I don't know how it can be said
except paradoxically:
What we see as sky or cloud is
what we have previously chosen to name it.

2.

You walked to Calvary,
the place of the skull
just outside Jerusalem's wall,
and I turned away,
returning in memory
to the tree of our meeting,
hoping to find its rhythm again,
the contour of its movement against the sky,
the strength of its roots in the earth.
And there I sat, paralyzed against its trunk,
waiting for something to happen without me,
waiting for you to come and find me again.

Something drove me inside
to the tree's image,
some inner compulsion that said
I had to realign myself with a movement
deep inside trees,
that said surrendering to their roots and trunks and branches

would enable you to find me when you came again.
Everything seemed out of joint,
and I knew that nothing we could do
would bring things back into place again.
We, like everything else that lives,
had somehow to find our inner movement once more.

I did not know it then, but in that movement
we would find you
as you rose from the dead,
through the deep roots of the tree
that held your lifeless body
high against the darkened sky.
You would rise in us
as if from some invisible root
that reaches down through our bodies
into the Garden we were banished from
when Yahweh found us standing beside another tree,
ashamed of our nakedness.

And so I sat and dreamed
the fig tree night and day,
until the morning of your rising
when we were all called together
to wait in the upper room.
I remember thinking that
we should be waiting by some tree.
The room, of course, was better
for your return
for that is where you said good-bye
to those of us gathered to eat
the Paschal meal.
You would find us again as *Church*
in the breaking of the bread;

you would find us as *individuals* beneath the tree
of our abandoning you.

So I sat beneath the tree
waiting for you to return and take away
the shame of my soul, naked before you.
You had done it before,
three days of years ago.
You would do it again
as I descended with you into the earth
toward that Paradise whose geography
is the human heart redeemed.

3.

In hiding I watched you
walk heavily to Calvary.
Now I watch you walk through doors
though you appear as substantial
as when you walked lightly upon the water
though you weighed, I'm sure,
as much as I do now.

Is your risen body the same body as mine
which now aches against this tree?
The same body, light though heavy,
and heavy with presence,
yet able to slip between the grains of wood
into the room where Thomas the Dullard
places his hand into your side
and feels the flesh parting

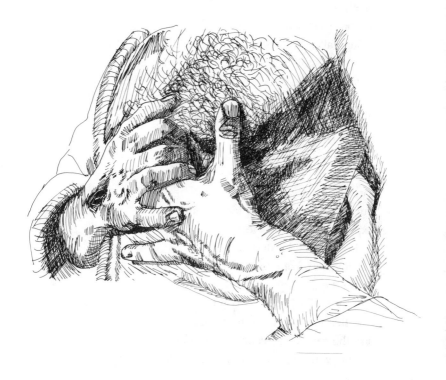

and the slick blood upon his fingertips?
If your hand now
is the same hand that beckoned me,
then everything we have believed is true,
and we are made whole
in your resurrection from the dead.

It must be so,
for we are without imagination
to dream so perfect a dream
of who you have become in saving us,
death revealing your immortality,
as you promised it would,
though all of us forgot what you said
almost as soon as the words passed your lips.
In your glorified body we are made whole,
brought together so perfectly
that we can pass freely through all of creation
as you have passed through the closed doors
separating us from creation.
And without you we live eternally fragmented,
forever disintegrating,
our whole being an exploding universe,
experiencing for all eternity
its being pulled asunder.
To die apart from you
is to be pulled apart from ourselves
and from all of creation contained within us.
And the tension between the fragments
and the center that cannot hold them
is what you meant by sin that leads to real death.

How extraordinary this passage of yours
through doors you used to make in that Nazareth workshop!
Is this then the real craft you were learning there,
the penetration of, the passage through?
Is this what moved you to state so grandly once,
"The Son cannot do anything at his own pleasure.
He can only do what he sees his Father doing;
what the Father does is what the Son does in his turn"?
Though I see it only vaguely, I think it was.

What is solid,
what is worked by human hands,
is somehow penetrable by the human person
raised to life in you and through you.
And now your Spirit has penetrated even my tough skull
so that I am thinking thoughts like these,
not knowing how I am thinking them.
And yet how relieved I am
that I can still think at all,
after what happened in Jerusalem
on that wood I thought to be impenetrable.
But hanging there, I now see,
gave you the passageway through
the very wood that killed you.

Wood, always wood with you,
from that stable you were born in,
to the shavings on the floor
where you worked as a boy into manhood,
to the boat you preached from,
to the tree you found me under,
to the tables you overturned in the Temple
and later ate from at the Passover meal,
to the crossed beams you carried to Calvary,
to the doors from which you emerged
into the room where everyone shivered
behind the wood that reminded them
of the narrow door to Paradise.
Little did we know when you were with us
how narrow that door really is
and what must happen to us
before we can slip between the grains of wood
into the glory of emergence.

4.

What we knew at first
was only what was *not* there in the tomb.
Your body was nowhere to be found.
The women who went to the tomb
to anoint your body with spices and ointments
said they found the stone rolled away
and, when they entered it,
they could not find your body.
And then two angels appeared to them
as men in dazzling clothes and said,

"Why do you seek the living among the dead?
Remember how he told you, while he was still in Galilee,
that the Son of Man must be delivered
into the hands of sinful men and be crucified,
and on the third day rise."

My reaction to the women's report
was typical of me then.
I remarked how fitting it was
that now we were supposed to believe,
purely on negative testimony,
that you had risen from the dead.
Once again God is present by his absence,
by what we don't see,
by what is not there.
The whole scenario fit my skepticism perfectly.
From the beginning
we were asked to believe in things we couldn't see or hear,
in a God who was a Spirit like the wind
which blew where it would and was known
only as it passed invisibly among us.

Or we were expected to believe
that you were the Messiah,
the Son of God,
though we saw so much humanness in you.
Always the same,
faith resting on what was not there,
not seen,
while what was seen and heard
proclaimed the opposite
of what we were supposed to believe.
How I longed for some confirmation
that what had happened three years before,

beneath the tree of my becoming,
was in fact what I thought it was
and not some mere coincidence.

What had happened to you and among us
from the hour of your betrayal by Judas
to the moment of the women announcing
that the tomb was empty of your body
was too great a trial of our faith
to be reversed by the negative testimony
of the women who loved you.
After all, the authorities had every reason
to remove your body by night,
lest your tomb become the shrine
and rallying point of the stories
they sought to discredit.
Besides, our sorely tested souls
would never base our belief
that you had risen from the dead on our inability
to find the body that Joseph of Arimathea
claimed to have removed from the cross,
wrapped in a linen shroud,
and laid in a rock-hewn tomb
without the proper anointing
because it was the Day of Preparation,
and the Sabbath was beginning.

And that is why I have now risen
from the day and night of this tree
and walked down to the shore of the lake
where we saw you on the shore as alive and human
as when we walked the same shore together
and you were fit and well,
robust in your young manhood,

eager for sharing Yahweh's word.
A word you never wrote down
lest it become Law like Moses' words to us;
A Word you kept living out in your person,
forcing us to keep our eyes on you,
knowing that it was you who had to convince us,
not what you had to say.
You were the Word.

We believed it then;
we know it now that we have seen you
walking upon the shore.
And everything the Word became in you
came together as you knelt upon the rocky shore
and built a fire and cooked the fish
and gave it to us to eat with bread.
You did upon the ground by the Sea of Galilee
what you did upon the hill of Calvary.
And we understood what you were doing
and knew we would do the same
whenever we met to eat the meal
and drink the wine consumed
in memory of you.

You were really writing the Word in the earth
where it belongs, as you had done before,
that day they brought to you the woman caught in adultery
for you to pronounce your Father's word of judgment
and you surprised us all by writing it in the dirt
where alone it can be found.
And now, Lord Jesus, you reconfirm on the ground by the sea
what happened on the bare ground of Bethlehem,
what was consummated as your blood fell
upon the soil of Calvary,

and what rose out of the dark ground that Sunday
the women went looking for you in the earth.

5.

Jesus by the sea,
you blow upon the embers of a little seaside fire
and the flame is rekindled,
and your breath moves over the land
onto the dark water
where we bob up and down watching our nets:
Simon Peter and Thomas "the Twin,"
the sons of Zebedee and two other disciples,
and I who now stand here alone
trying to remember how it was.

It comes back to me clearly,
as if everything that day is illumined
by your bright presence on the beach
that has become these words,
becoming now
my own canticle:

> You sit by the sea,
> small fire and one fish
> and no clouds
> aflame with angels.
> You wait for us
> to row toward you
> your human hand
> stirring embers.

And you're revealed again
when we partake of food,
the skeleton of whose name
becomes your signature.
The fisherman is at last the fish
and we the fishers of God.

6.

A place of land and water and you
and the wind, always the wind blowing.
That is where we left you standing,
once more sending us away from the sea and our boats
moored where the water meets the land.
We had thought that it was over
and knew nothing of what to do,
except return to boats and water.

"I am going fishing," Peter said,
and we went with him down to the Sea of Galilee
and caught nothing that night
and it seemed like those former times of boredom
when fishing was all there was
and my only refuge was daydreaming
and withdrawal into my own mind.
No one said as much,
but we all were acting
as though the past three years
were but an interlude,
a fisherman's brief adventure on land,
something to remember on long nights

and longer days
as we sat watching the net-floats bob,
mesmerizing strained eyes.

We were back to who we used to be,
and we did not really expect
that you would once again stand on the shore
and ask us to follow you and send us forth.
But you did,
and this time it was even more mysterious than the first;
for as you sent us inland again,
we turned to wave
and you suddenly dissolved into sea-mist
where you stood,
and we saw nothing but boats and water
and the smoldering fire you had built upon the sand.

7.

Tree-roots in the sand.
Wind and water meeting trees and land.
The memory never fades.
There is only your bright presence
emerging from and dissolving into sea-mist,
your bright feet ascending from Mount Olivet into the cloud,
only your bright Spirit returning
with the sound of a mighty wind,
filling the house where we are sitting.
And there appear to us tongues as of fire,
and they rest upon each one of us,
and we are filled with your Holy Spirit.

And we become the wind in which you move
through the branches of the trees,
over land and water,
making all things new.
And I,
even I,
am the stuff of wind and fire.

EPILOGUE

And so I leave you, Nathanael,
in your marble sarcophagus
beneath the altar of your church
on this island in the Tiber.
In a final irony
even your name has been erased
and you have become a perhaps-apostle.
Nathanael, found beneath a fig tree in Galilee,
now you are Bartholomew,
skinned, floating in the Tiber
between Trastevere and the great Jewish synagogue of Rome.

I have knelt this morning at your tomb
(wondering if it *is* your tomb)
to take my leave,
to ask your intercession: that
through you, Saint Bartholomew,
I might somehow find my way back
to the tree of Nathanael,
and know the journey you made
from Galilee to Rome and back again
to the tree near the shore of the sea.

Murray Bodo, O.F.M.
St. Bartholomew's Church
Rome, Isola Tiberina